Alan Billings is an Anglican parish p[...] tor of the Centre for Ethics and Reli[...] Before that he was a priest in inner-ci[...] Deputy Leader of the City Council; Vice Principal of Ripon College, Cuddesdon; and Principal of the West Midlands Ministerial Training Course, Birmingham. He was a member of the Archbishop's Commission on Urban Priority Areas, which produced the report *Faith in the City* in 1985, and the Community Cohesion Panel of the Home Office, set up by the government following the disturbances in Bradford, Oldham and Burnley in 2001. He is a member of the Youth Justice Board for England and Wales and a contributor to 'Thought for the Day' on BBC Radio 4.

Also by Alan Billings and published by SPCK

Dying and Grieving – A Guide to Pastoral Ministry

Secular Lives, Sacred Hearts

The role of the Church in
a time of no religion

Alan Billings

First published in Great Britain in 2004 by
Society for Promoting Christian Knowledge
36 Causton Street
London SW1P 4AU

British Library Cataloguing-in-Publication Data
A catalogue record for this book is available from the British Library

ISBN 0–281–05704–4

1 3 5 7 9 10 8 6 4 2

Typeset by Avocet Typeset, Chilton, Aylesbury, Bucks
Printed in Great Britain by Bookmarque Ltd, Croydon, Surrey

For Hugh, Guy, Laura and Rufus

And I awoke and found me here
On the cold hill's side.
John Keats

Contents

Acknowledgements

This book arose out of conversations with members of the ministerial team at St George's, Kendal – Jean Radley, Peter Smith, Liz Hawker, Brian Stabler, Val Carradus, Arnold Brockbank, Dorothy Dawes, Peter Dudek, Ken Tulley and Jean Edmondson. Ideas were refined as a result of conversations with former Cuddesdon students, now ordained, who have remained friends – Gary Lewis, Andrew Studdert Kennedy, Viv Armstrong-MacDonnell, Jeremy and Ellen Clark-King (who gave me half the title) – and members of the Centre for Practical Christianity, Kendal – Hilary Binks, Elizabeth Hawthorne and Brian Stabler. I thank them for the generous way they have shared their time, thoughts and experience with me over the years, though they did not anticipate that what we talked about might be turned into a book, and should not be held responsible for what is said here.

Introduction

I wrote this book because I wanted to encourage fellow Christians, lay and ordained, to think again about the role of the Church in contemporary society. It is very easy to feel discouraged when confronted with the statistics of numerical decline. Yet this is invariably the starting point for sociological and cultural commentary whenever religion in Britain is discussed, if religion is discussed at all. But the conventional analysis of Britain's religious health has never seemed to me to do justice to my own experiences as a parish priest. I simply do not recognize what is so often served up as a sociological description of religion in Britain today. It leaves out crucial pieces of evidence and as a result is not sufficiently nuanced.

But if the analysis and description is not quite right we as a church are in danger of drawing the wrong lessons from that. Many of the contemporary strategies now being commended or simply assumed seem to me, therefore, to be based on a misdiagnosis of modern Britain.

I begin by reconsidering some of the evidence for religion in Part One. This leads me to suggest that a more accurate description of the British is to see them as 'culturally Christian' rather than as those who 'believe but do not belong' or as secular. If this is true, then it suggests a particular vocation for the Christian Church at the beginning of a new century: the Church should see an important part of its task as supporting and nourishing cultural Christianity. How is that to be done?

Cultural Christians do sometimes seek the ministry of the Church – most notably in the occasional offices. But what exactly is it that they seek? The astonishing thing is that we know so little about what people want of the Church. In Part Two, therefore, I try to tease out the reasons why people who are not regular churchgoers nevertheless seek ministry from the Church at certain points in their lives, principally at the birth of a child, when two people get married and when someone dies. What do they want and how far can the Church help them? In these chapters I make use of some small-scale research from my own parish.

Finally, in Part Three I try to draw all this together with some concluding remarks about the nature and task of the local church.

As the twenty-first century begins, the pressure is on the (mainstream) Church in Britain to abandon its traditional role as a focus of meaning embodied in a sacred building in each locality and to see itself more like a movement with no fixed abode. I write to encourage Christians to resist these pressures and rediscover the importance of the local church and the local ministry it offers.

Part One

The context: Cultural Christianity

Sacred hearts
The legacy of Christianity

*Father didn't care to which church he belonged, provided
he could stay away from it.*
William Woodruff, *The Road to Nab End*

The changing role of the clergy

In the twenty-first century very few people attend places of worship in the United Kingdom or seek out the ordained ministers of the Church. This is an aspect of the secularization of British society that has occurred during the course of my ôwn working life. When I was a young lay person in a church on a post-war council housing estate in the late 1950s, I observed parishioners knocking on the vicarage door on a daily basis. Managing time was a major preoccupation for my vicar. Uncritically, I assumed that this was how it always was and always would be. I had not foreseen a time when the social usefulness of the clergy would be called into question.

The social usefulness of the clergy

I had come from an Anglo-Catholic background and had read numerous accounts of the slum priests in the late nineteenth and early twentieth century. Their churches were at the centre of their local communities and their ministry was in constant demand. When some of them died, the whole community turned out to watch the funeral procession. These men – they were all men – were not ambitious for preferment but rather were committed to long ministries in their parishes; their lives were marked by great busyness. I read, for example, this account of a typical day for the unmarried clerical staff in the Parochial Mission House of St George in the East, London, in 1856:

> The first bell for rising was rung at 6.30 a.m.; we said Prime in the Oratory at 7; Mattins was said at 7.30, followed by the celebration of the Holy Eucharist. After breakfast, followed by Terce, the clergy and teachers went to their respective work – some in school, some in the study or district. Sext was said at 12.45, immediately before dinner, when the household again assembled ... After dinner, rest, letters, visiting, or school work, as the case might be, and then tea at 5.30. After tea, choir practice, classes, hearing confessions, or attending to special cases. Supper at 9.15, followed by Compline, when those who had finished their work returned to their rooms.[1]

This, I believed, was what ordained ministry was all about and I anticipated leading the sort of life they had led when I was ordained. I expected to be busy and to fall into bed exhausted but content each day. I even absorbed from the Revd Peter Green, Rector of Salford at the time of the First World War, the wisdom that a day-off was only essential for a 'man under forty':

> As a man grows older, and needs less active exercise than when young, and as his work develops in variety and interest, so that one piece of work is the relaxation and rest needed after some other piece, a day off each week may become unnecessary.[2]

However, by the time I came to a curacy in 1968 the situation had changed. By then, church attendance had fallen noticeably. Churches had begun to consolidate a range of morning services – Low and High Mass, or Sung Mattins and Holy Communion – into one Parish Communion or Family

Service. Mattins, Evensong and High Mass largely disappeared. The educated middle classes had begun to desert the Church of England in droves.

As attendances fell, so did the demand for the pastoral ministry of the clergy. People stopped knocking on vicarage doors for help or counsel. Why should they? The welfare state now catered for all their needs through a growing army of assorted social and welfare workers, professionally trained and with the resources of the local and national state to support them. Moreover, these professionals had no ulterior axe to grind – or so it seemed. Clerical help always came at a price: the clergy wanted your soul.

Regaining social usefulness

In the late 1960s, therefore, clergy as clergy ceased to be socially useful. As a consequence, clergy tried to regain value in two quite distinct ways. Evangelical clergy retreated into their own congregations. They abandoned the attempt to find a more general usefulness and concentrated on what they saw as the crucial tasks of ministry – building strong congregations of believing and committed Christians through a ministry of evangelism and teaching. In the more restricted contexts of their own congregations their ministry was valued and they were affirmed.

Clergy in the more Catholic or middle-of-the-road traditions chose a different path, seeking to regain social value by adapting the priestly role to that of one of the caring professions. Over the years there were changing fashions in this attempt to regain usefulness, as my own ministry bears out. In the 1970s, as a young priest in an inner-city parish, I practised a form of pastoral ministry that modelled itself on that of the social worker. In the theological college I had been taught what was then the new subject of pastoral studies by a social worker. She was anxious that clergy should have some proper professional discipline and some theoretical basis for what they did. So we read manuals of social care alongside George Herbert's *A Priest to the Temple*. I saw pastoral ministry in terms of one-to-one involvement with people in their homes and learnt to speak about the 'cases' with which I was dealing. I was as much concerned with people's struggles to make ends meet as with any overt spiritual needs. Or rather, I was persuaded that material and spiritual needs could not be separated out. Jesus fed the hungry body as well as the hungry soul. I must do the same. Indeed, such material concerns were really spiritual matters and since no one could reasonably be expected to spend much time thinking about the state of their soul if they had no job or the family home was full of damp, it was clear where my daily priorities had to be.

Gradually I came to see that the material well-being of individuals and their families depended on the general well-being of the community as a whole. How could mothers and fathers be expected to raise their children well if the local economy was not flourishing and the neighbourhood was starved of facilities – nurseries, playgrounds, safe streets – the list was a very long one. By the 1970s, therefore, I had turned to a greater involvement with the community and unconsciously adapted the clerical role to that of the community worker. I next came to realize that the community development in which I was deeply involved crucially depended on decisions made in the Town Hall. I was politicized as a consequence and became a ward councillor, remaining a leading member of Sheffield City Council as Deputy Leader and Chair of Finance throughout the Thatcher years.

These attempts to make pastoral ministry socially useful by adapting secular roles were reinforced by a number of different theologies that gave to what I did some doctrinal and scriptural underpinning. In the 1960s and 1970s there were forms of secular theology. Harvey Cox had praised the secular city and suggested that the function of the Church was to busy itself with such secular concerns as 'healing urban fractures'.[3] In the 1980s I was influenced by liberation theologians in both Latin America and the United Kingdom. I learnt to read the Bible politically and to speak about the kingdom of God as a political 'project'.[4] This broadened out in the 1990s to embrace issues of world poverty – Third World debt – and environmental concerns.[5]

By the end of the twentieth century, however, I had grown weary of the community models. Those people who had done well in the inner city – raising and educating their children, retraining and holding down jobs – had not necessarily become happier. Marriages still disintegrated, relationships remained sources of worry and people became depressed in the face of life's trials – unemployment, sickness, rejection and bereavement. However much the local neighbourhood was transformed, these human problems remained. The socially valuable work now seemed to be that of the counsellor and therapist. I adapted my clerical role accordingly. But as with all the other secular models the question remained: why should anyone seek out an ordained minister when the secular counsellor would do the job just as well if not better and without demanding anything in return?

At each stage of my own transformation I was also influencing a congregation along similar or supportive lines. The themes of sermons and intercessions, the projects and concerns of the Church reflected my own changing interests and priorities.

We should not despise this drive for social usefulness or think of it as new. When we look back over previous centuries we can see that the clergy, especially Anglican clergy, have played any number of roles. They have been school teachers, law enforcement officers, dispensers of charity, physicians, registrars and so on. Most of these roles were stripped from the clergy during the course of the nineteenth century as each of these tasks became the prime responsibility of discrete professions. What happened in the latter half of the twentieth century was merely the continuation of an older tradition, but adapting it to changing circumstances.

Since the 1960s, then, clergy have been tempted to become social workers, community workers, politicians, community development workers and counsellors. But, in the early years of the twenty-first century, most clergy report that they have few callers at the vicarage and filling time is more the issue than finding time.

This, then, is the starting-point for any consideration of pastoral ministry today: the clergy are rarely asked for, and so seek social usefulness either by retreating within the life of their own congregation or by adapting the pastoral role to one that is considered valuable by a secular society.

When ministry is sought

But if people no longer seek the ministry of the Church on a regular basis in any numbers, on those occasions when they do, it becomes a matter of some significance. Christian people ought to think carefully about why, at particular moments, or in certain circumstances, ministry is asked for or becomes possible. Although these occasions may on the face of it be a continuation of ministry that has been offered in all previous centuries, their significance changes as we move ever deeper into a time of no religion. The surprising thing is that, as far as I am aware, little attempt has been made to discover what moves people to turn to the Church when they do. In the absence of hard evidence, those of us who offer ministry at the parish level must make best guesses. This, then, is an extended best guess. I ask the question: in what circumstances and for what reasons do people who are not regular members of Christian congregations ask for acts of Christian ministry? Then, in the light of that, we can consider how we might improve our response.

As a way of proceeding this may seem unexceptional. But it is not how the Church usually operates. Take requests for infant baptism. Those involved in preparation for baptism will usually be concerned to explain to families what the rite means from the Church's perspective: an act of initiation, promises about conduct, belief and church membership, and so on. It would be rare to begin the other way round and ask what the family is wanting from baptism – except as a prelude to telling them what they ought to want! It might even be considered rather presumptuous or even blasphemous to ask them. Yet there is something discordant here. If ministry is about meeting a pastoral need by making the grace of God concrete for people, we surely have some obligation to understand as far as we can what those needs are, even when it is a sacrament of the Church that is being sought. The task will not be easy. There is little research evidence, and British people are notoriously reluctant to discuss such concerns.

The only way I can proceed is by generalizing from my own context. That is multi-layered. There is the broad cultural context of a secular nation state in western Europe in the early twenty-first century. There is also my more immediate context: my parish. During the course of these chapters I shall move between the two. In order to earth the discussion I shall give a brief description of both – first the broad cultural context and then the parish. The people whose lives I go on to describe are the flesh and blood people of this time and place. In doing this I am only doing what every minister of the gospel unconsciously does all the time as he seeks to be a pastor to a particular group of people. But sometimes we need to do the work of contextual analysis a little more explicitly.

Religion and society

Before I turn more specifically to my parish of St George's, Kendal, a word of explanation is needed for a distinction I make between 'institutional' or 'church Christianity' and 'cultural Christianity'. What are the realities that this distinction is pointing us towards?

Religion in the wider context

In 1892, just before he died, the poet Alfred, Lord Tennyson, wondered what the future held for religion. 'Do you think they will give up all religious forms and go and sit in silence in churches listening to the organs?'[6] I spoke above of these days as a 'time of no religion'. But that is only true if our measure of religion is church attendance. What I will suggest is that although churchgoing has declined, people are still influenced by the Christian faith; they have an emotional attachment to it even though they have little time for the finer points of doctrine or church attendance. To that extent they should still be considered Christian – a designation many would not want to repudiate. However, there is a considerable debate amongst sociologists and social commentators around these issues. Although most would agree that the British people are less rather than more religious than we were, important questions remain where the jury, as the Americans say, is still out: how less religious are we? What marks have the centuries of Christian faith left on the culture generally, and how long will they continue to have influence?

The evidence is not straightforward and there are many gaps in our knowledge. Much depends on what you measure and where you start. But we are in danger of being entirely seduced by a 'strong' version of the concept of secularization – the idea that as societies modernize they tend to abandon religion. The 'strong' version maintains that there is something inexorable and irresistible about modernity and religious decline. But how secure is the 'strong' version of secularization theory?

On the one hand, churchgoing has suffered a considerable decline, especially over the second half of the twentieth century, and few would dispute that. As far as the Church of England is concerned, the collapse of its middle-class constituency has been dramatic and is well documented. The loss of younger women from the late 1950s was particularly serious, not just because women have been the mainstay of congregations, but because as they had families they were then less likely to induct the next generation into the faith. The loss of children at that time led directly to the loss of all subsequent generations. We can trace this downward spiral in the decline of the Sunday School movement. As late as 1957, 76 per cent of people over 30 years of age had attended Sunday School at some time in their life. But by the 1970s Sunday Schools had ceased to exist in many churches and have not enjoyed much of a revival since.[7] Whether the losses spell terminal decline, as some have predicted, is more debatable: the Church has considerable resources and the fall in numbers is not uniform across the different types of Anglicanism. But there will undoubtedly be some very painful reconfiguring of the Church of England in the coming decades as it finds its commitment to every part of the country increasingly hard to sustain. Neither the Roman Catholic Church nor the other Protestant churches have the same compulsion to be present in every place, so their decline is being better managed. Overall it does mean that the Christian Church may be reduced to fewer and fewer, mainly urban and suburban centres. But if the starting point for assessing the place of religion in Britain today is with numbers of active members, the message of decline cannot be disputed. Moreover, this is in spite of considerable efforts at evangelism during the final decade of the last century. The inescapable message of the twentieth century was that the British people do not want to attend churches on a regular basis and there is no strategy of either evangelism or church restructuring that can make a significant difference to that.

On the other hand, the 2001 census tells another story – or at least sounds a note of caution if we want to speak of Britain as a secular society. Over 76 per cent of people, answering a question that was not compulsory, identified themselves with a faith tradition.[8] That is a very large proportion of the population and suggests that religion has a continuing and significant influence. Those faith traditions now encompass more than Christianity and Judaism. Among the most vibrant urban faith groups are Muslims, Hindus and Sikhs, whose age profile suggests that they will be able to sustain themselves for at least the rest of the present century. They may even become the majority in terms of active faith membership. Alternative forms of spirituality, sometimes called 'New Age', are probably not significant numerically, but they do indicate that some people may be 'spiritual' without being members of a faith community and they do point to the fact that more and more people are willing to draw from different traditions to help them in their spiritual quest.[9] However, the majority of people probably think of themselves as broadly Christian, even though they are not church attenders and even though they are becoming ever more eclectic.

These people think of Christianity more in terms of praxis – a way of living – than a set of beliefs. They live Christian lives; they are Christians because their lives reflect the life and values of Jesus Christ. Like him they acknowledge that we live in a creation, that God cares for us, that we should care for one another, and so on. It is the religion of the golden rule: do unto others as you would have them do to you. Sometimes they feel the need to attend a church on such occasions as a Christmas Carol Service or Midnight Mass. They want family weddings and funerals to be held at a church. They watch and feel uplifted by *Songs of Praise* on Sunday-night television. Sometimes they might want to hear inspiring music at a cathedral Mattins or Evensong. They see the Church, in other words, as a spiritual resource. But they do not want to belong.[10]

At least I think this is what motivates them, and it is how I make sense of what people tell me; but the truth is that we know next to nothing about what the 90 per cent of people who do not attend places of worship regularly actually do think, believe or feel about religion. They are not the subject of research. But if our starting point for assessing religion in this country is with non-institutional as well as institutional forms, we must hesitate before describing Britain as wholly secular. They may not belong and they may not be greatly believing; but Christianity for all of us is about a way of life, a praxis, as much as it is about churchgoing or saying the creed. For the majority of British people their praxis is Christian and they have said, through the census, that this is part of their self-definition. They have rejected the label 'secular' and we should respect that, starting with the Church – and the professional sociologists!

Cultural Christianity

Although few now attend church on any regular basis, and urban Britain has mosques, temples, synagogues and gurdwaras as well as churches, it still makes sense to speak of the general cultural context of British society as Christian – in the same way that we would want to call, for example, the countries of the middle east Islamic.[11] The tide of faith may have turned, as Matthew Arnold recognized in the nineteenth century, but as it ebbs it leaves its mark. We are a society that has been deeply influenced by the Christian religion and that will be true for a very long time to come, even if the number of churchgoers does not increase significantly. Britain is culturally Christian.

This raises the interesting theological question of whether you can be Christian wholly outside the Church. Members of churches, especially the clergy, would be horrified at such a suggestion; but many people in this country – as the census bears out – insist that they are Christians even though they never attend church. I think this means that sociologically we have to identify two types of Christianity now in Britain. On the one hand there are those who do attend churches – there is 'church Christianity'; on the other hand, there are those who live by Christian values and believe in God but who do not see the need to be in church every week or even at all – there is 'cultural Christianity', the legacy of church Christianity.

Can we say any more about 'cultural Christianity'? Cultural Christianity is the effect of a thousand years of Christianity in these islands. That has left behind a legacy of stories, words, images, values and a morality. It has influenced every aspect of life, high culture as well as popular. The world of classical music and art is saturated with the language and imagery of the Christian faith – from Handel's *Messiah* to Stanley Spencer's *Resurrection in Cookham*. But popular culture can just as easily make reference to eating forbidden fruit or being a Judas. The way we treat one another – especially the sick, the aged, the poor, the stranger in our midst – owes a great deal to the biblical notion that all people are created in God's image and deserving of care. We are a people who have been shaped and continue to live by Christian values. In that sense, Christianity has triumphed; the culture is Christian.

But can this cultural legacy continue to influence? How is it sustained? How does it continue to be refreshed and reapplied? These are the key questions and they point us to a continuing role for the Church (as well as the school), though the role is not one that the clergy are particularly well trained for and not one all would accept. This role, however – keeping Christian language and imagery before people – may have to be done in more imaginative and less ecclesiastically based ways in the future, and the role of lay people may be critical.

For instance, in 2000 I went to see an exhibition of Christian art and artefacts at the National Gallery called 'Seeing Salvation'. The Gallery was packed. Visitors were young and old, men and women. In his introduction in the catalogue, the director of the Gallery, Neil MacGregor, had speculated that some visitors might find it hard to appropriate the pictures since so many now were no longer practising members of the Church. He need not have worried. Many people to whom I subsequently spoke about the exhibition had not been or were no longer members of the Church but they had been touched by it. The story of Christ lies deep within all of us. I was moved to hear one woman speak about sitting in front of a painting of the suffering Christ by Velázquez, quietly sobbing. She said she was not moved simply by the image of a suffering man. It was a suffering man; but what made the painting moving for her was that this suffering man was also the Christ. We can reappropriate and refresh the vision, the language and the imagery of Christianity, though for many it may have to be beyond the formal setting of parish churches – except for those rare occasions when ministry is sought.

Perhaps here we need to note the importance of early induction into the Christian tradition. Shortly before his death, D. H. Lawrence wrote about how the hymns of his non-conformist childhood had become an enduring part of his consciousness and stayed with him all his life. Although he repudiated Christian doctrine, lines from those hymns continued to exercise an influence.[12]

A time of no religion?

It is, then, these seeming contradictions that enable some to claim that religion is in terminal decline, that its disappearance is only a matter of time, while others can speak of religion, or faith or spirituality, as still live options, though not necessarily anchored in organized groups. What we can say is perhaps best summarized in a series of statements:

- There has been a severe haemorrhaging of membership from the churches in the past 50 years.
- Within the overall decline, charismatic or evangelical types of Christianity have grown where others have withered.
- Much of the energy of mainstream churches will be taken up managing decline.
- Successive waves of immigration in the post-war period have led to the appearance of new faith communities that are now among the most active groups.
- Many people would regard themselves as open to the possibility of the spiritual but would not wish to be members of any particular religious group.[13]
- There are two Christianities: 'church Christianity' and 'cultural Christianity'.
- 'Cultural Christianity' is non-credal and non-attending – a legacy of the time of 'church Christianity' – and is more concerned with praxis than belief.
- The real religious views, attitudes and sensibilities of the majority of people are largely unknown; we simply do not have enough detailed evidence.

Religion in the local context

Let me now turn from the national picture to the more local context of a particular town and parish. The reason for doing this is to make the point that what constitutes 'religion' and 'ministry' is crucially dependent on the particular circumstances of time and place. I will describe my patch, but each minister must similarly seek to understand his or her own.

Kendal is a small English market town of some 26,000 people at the southern edge of the Lake District National Park. Its population is almost uniformly white with few members of ethnic minorities. It is increasingly dependent on tourism and related industries as farming and manufacturing have declined. It is also becoming popular as a good place for retirement. The town bursts with voluntary clubs and societies. St George's parish is at the northern end of the town and serves a mainly working-class and lower-middle-class population. The housing is a mix of modest owner occupation and rented accommodation, private and public. Baptism registers record the occupations of parents and from them a picture emerges of people in various blue-collar and mainly non-professional white-collar jobs: warehouseman, HGV driver, storeman, plasterer, soldier, ambulance driver, shop assistant, cook, nursery nurse, receptionist, care worker.[14] There are as many unmarried couples as married. There is the occasional single parent, usually the mother.

The town is still a centre for the surrounding farming communities. A number of businesses have an agricultural connection and there is an auction mart (in St George's parish), though business was severely disrupted by the foot-and-mouth crisis in 2001. But in recent years some traditional industries have been lost: K shoes, AXA insurance. The future of manufacturing, and the unskilled jobs it provided, looks somewhat bleak.

The majority of people in St George's parish are from local Cumbrian families; few have moved to Kendal from more distant parts of the country. In this respect there is some contrast with other town parishes, where a considerable number of people are newcomers. Some have moved to the town to work but many have come to retire. But these are the new generation of retired people. They have money, they have hobbies and interests, they have energy, they are mobile and they have time. Native Kendalians watch with some astonishment at the way in which the newcomers (they are referred to as 'offcomers') set about moulding the town in their image. They are soon involved in local clubs and societies and where a group does not currently exist to meet their recreational and other needs they form one. They also join churches and soon find themselves in positions of influence and leadership. In St George's congregation many of the new initiatives have come from just such people.

There is a perception in some parts of the country that churchgoing is much stronger in country towns like Kendal than elsewhere. In fact, 8 per cent of the population of Kendal attends churches and chapels each Sunday, and this is roughly the proportion for the country as a whole. Like most people, Kendalians are not hostile to organized religion; they are indifferent, or at least they are indifferent most of the time. They do not attend church and they do not discuss religion with their family or friends. If they do have religious thoughts or spiritual experiences, they largely keep them to themselves. Some mainly middle-aged women seek spiritual experiences in alternative practices – such as yoga or meditation – but they are very small in number. It is very hard to say whether indifference is leading to the religious equivalence of being musically tone deaf. In other words, do people who are indifferent to religion eventually become incapable of having anything like a religious or spiritual experience? Over time, does indifference shut down some vital faculty, so that reviving it becomes progressively more difficult?

But religion – or perhaps the church – has its uses. There are some occasions when the church can be visited – for weddings, baptisms and funerals, on Remembrance Day or at Christmas or Harvest or Mothering Sunday. But not every week. On the whole, however, people do seem glad and perhaps even grateful that the church is there and that some people support it on a regular basis. It is just that most Kendalians do not see the need themselves to be frequent attenders.[15]

Professional sociologists of religion have described this phenomenon variously as 'believing without belonging' or 'vicarious religion' or 'differential religion'. I am calling it 'cultural Christianity': it is lived or lived-out Christianity. It is hardly 'believing without belonging', since most people are not much interested in beliefs; the attachment is more emotional and practical than intellectual – having a sacred heart. But it is related to historic Christianity. This is why in the census, for example, they had no difficulty in identifying with the Christian tradition, and why from time to time, particularly at times of change in life, the ministry of the Church and clergy can be sought.

But why? Clergy tend to think about what people may need or be looking for in terms of beliefs. If someone brings a baby for baptism we want to explore with them what they believe about baptism. Then we become anxious if they seem unable or even unwilling to talk about their beliefs. So we question their motives. I believe a more fruitful approach is to think about these requests for ministry in terms of other kinds of needs, in particular the need to be able to manage change. This is to adopt, at least initially, a more sociological or socio-psychological approach.

What all this suggests is that in this time of cultural Christianity we need to think again about the role of the Church towards those who still regard themselves as Christian but do not want to attend church. The vocation of church members in this time of cultural Christianity is both more modest and more challenging than we thought: it is about how we sustain people in their praxis.

Summary

What I have sought to suggest in this first chapter is this. As a nation we have largely stopped attending church: in that sense this is a time of no religion and we lead secular lives. But we have not ceased to be spiritual beings and we are still influenced by the Christian legacy: most of us are 'cultural Christians' – we still have sacred hearts. The Church has a choice: it can continue to be the Church of the nation by trying to keep that legacy alive or it can turn its back by turning inward and becoming one more religious sect along the high street. Opportunities for renewing the Christian legacy occur when the ministry of the Church is sought. This happens at baptisms, weddings and funerals, and when people in a particular place and in certain circumstances become aware of themselves as a community and turn to the Church for specific ministry. They did this, for example, when the two children, Jessica Chapman and Holly Wells were abducted in the Cambridgeshire town of Soham in August 2002. The local church provided a space, a language and some ritual in which grief could be articulated and in which some articulation of meaning attempted; this was possible because the nation remains culturally Christian. If the Church is to maintain this pastoral role its members need to puzzle out why people who do not attend services on a regular basis sometimes seek ministry – making concrete the grace of God – and how they can shape it better to meet pastoral needs. I turn to that next and also consider what I believe are some of the threats to that ministry in contemporary society.

~2~

Secular lives
Ministry in a time of no religion

And will they cast the altars down,
Scatter the chalice, crush the bread?
In field, in village, and in town
He hides an unregarded head . . .
Alice Meynell, 'In Portugal'

Threats to ministry in contemporary society

I have characterized the present as a time of no religion. More precisely, for at least the past 40 years of the twentieth century, people in Britain (and throughout western Europe) have been walking away from *organized* religion. Although the majority still want to call themselves 'Christian', and the culture remains indelibly marked with Christianity, most people are living their lives with diminishing reference to the beliefs and practices of the churches. But what, if anything, is taking the place of religion? What gives contemporary people their sense of purpose? Where do people find the resources they need to face life's challenges and crises? How are we to understand the developing secular culture of Britain?

Alternatives to religion

At one time we might have thought that alternative political ideologies that resembled religions – Fascism, Marxism or socialism – might supersede religion as the source of meaning; but a century of ideological conflicts has left people as disillusioned with politics as they are indifferent to organized religion.[1] There has been a walking away from ideology and politics as well as from religion. People have turned in quite a different direction for meaning. This turn has been identified as a turn inward. What we have witnessed over the past half century has been a turn away from all external sources of meaning and authority and a 'turn to the self'.

Table 1: Focus of human concerns

Period	Pre-modern	Modern	Post-modern
Human concern	God/the supernatural	Humanity/nature	Self
Authority	Scriptures/Church	Scientific reason	Emotional self
Experts	Priest/theologian	Scientist	Therapist/counsellor
Attitudes to time	The destroyer	Progress	Present moment

As we look back over the centuries of human history, we can see some very large shifts in human concerns (see Table 1). In particular we can see a shift from concern for God and the supernatural (which typified the pre-modern period) to a concern for the world (beginning with the Renaissance, then decisively at the Enlightenment – the modern period);[2] now the concern has shifted to the self (the post-modern turn). The gaze of human beings has shifted from up (to God), to around (the world), to within (the self).

Each of these shifts of concern is associated with the acceptance of different authorities for settling the question of how we are to live. When God was the focus, the place where God revealed himself was authoritative – and that was the Scriptures, with the Church as the interpreter of the Scriptures. As the focus shifted to the world, people looked to the empirical sciences. But the new authority is the individual self. Who else could be expert or knowledgeable in the matter of your emotional well-being apart from you?

We can notice also a shift in the way the passage of time has been understood.[3] When life was nasty, brutish and short – in the pre-modern period – time was often feared as the great destroyer. If life were to improve, this would have to come through God's intervention. In the modern period, as Western nations prospered and people lived longer, time was opportunity. Human beings could make a difference by setting goals and achieving longer-term ends; we could entertain the idea of progress and work for causes that might not come to pass in our life-time. With the turn to the self, it is the present moment that has become important.

The contemporary emphasis on emotion

The turn to the self has meant that ours is a culture that takes the interior, emotional life of the individual very seriously. For many, emotional well-being has become the goal of life, and people make sense of the world through the prism of emotion. Anything that threatens the emotional well-being of the individual, particularly the individual's sense of self-worth, is regarded as the greatest of evils. Unfortunately, quite a lot threatens self-esteem, including some of life's most everyday occurrences – setbacks, failures, rejections and disappointments of every kind. This has led to the human condition being described in modern culture as 'vulnerable'. We are vulnerable people whose feelings of self-worth can be so easily damaged – and damaged for life. So attending to our emotional well-being is life's key task. We need to know how to recognize our feelings, or release our feelings, or manage our feelings. This is a task that people must undertake for themselves, though they may be helped by those who have expertise in dealing with emotions – therapists and counsellors. We may also need to go further and discover the 'real' or 'true' self, the self that lies deep within us, the self that has been suppressed by family or society. That task may involve learning some technique of self-discovery and thence self-improvement – hence some of the New Age practices and practitioners.

As a result of this turn to the self, in the words of Frank Furedi, 'the language of emotionalism pervades popular culture, the world of politics, the workplace, schools and universities and every day life.'[4] Furedi could also have included the churches in his list since they too have embraced emotionalism – and, indeed, the only part of the Church that is growing is that which captures the *Zeitgeist* by emphasizing feelings, namely, the Charismatic and Pentecostal movements.[5] These churches combine a concern for the transcendent God with practices that play to individual emotion. People feel good about themselves after worship, and what the non-Charismatic visitor to such services notices most of all is how everything centres on the emotions of the worshippers, even though the language is about God.

Every aspect of life is now described in terms of what we might call 'therapeutic language' – medical–psychological language. So, workers do not fail to organize their time and activities sensibly, they are 'stressed out'. Inconsiderate motorists are in the grip of 'road rage'. Children in school are no longer badly behaved, they have 'attention deficit'. If things go wrong, we are 'devastated'. If we are criticized, we suffer 'low self-esteem'. As the therapeutic imagination has extended, more and more quite ordinary and seemingly innocent situations have come to be seen as potentially damaging. The relationships of teacher and child, parent and child, the family, marriage – all have had the spotlight on them as sites of danger and damage. No human experience, however unlikely, can now be considered immune to emotional catastrophe: a new help-line, for example, called 'Fathers Matter' was established in 2004 to assist men suffering from post-natal depression.[6] We are even beginning to transfer therapeutic language from the individual to the collective, so that a whole town might be 'traumatized' and need 'healing' or need to have 'confidence-building measures' put in place.[7]

Behind this is the suggestion that individuals are emotionally extremely fragile, easily 'traumatized' – by abusive relationships or terrible experiences. Once this psychological damage has been inflicted on us, we may be scarred for a life-time. Then we need help, but not from family or friends, but from professionals who know what needs to be done – the therapists and counsellors.[8]

Some commentators have called this the culture of narcissism or the culture of emotionalism.[9] I prefer to speak of a therapeutic culture since what I am concerned about here – the

way the culture is becoming soaked in the vocabulary of emotion and feelings – has been very much mediated through therapists and counsellors and the whole of that therapeutic
industry (which increasingly includes priests and ministers).

We can trace the triumph of this therapeutic sensibility to the
final decades of the last century. Prior to that, the emotional life
of people was generally thought to be a private matter and
managed organically through membership of families and
other small communities, including church fellowships. We
lived then in traditional communities, where individual lives
were lived out with considerable reference to the norms and
expectations of the community. Traditional communities told
you how to live – as a single man or woman, as a husband or
wife, as a parent or child – and passed on the received wisdom
about how to do it well. Modern life militates against such
community living. This is the result of both private choice – we
want to live more individualistic lives, and prosperity enables
us to do it – and social and economic trends, which lead to
more compartmentalized lives in which work, residence and
leisure are separated out.

When we did live in more close-knit, traditional communities,
we tended to admire those who kept their feelings to themselves
and maintained a stiff upper lip in the face of adversity. There
was something noble and heroic about the person who
remained cheerful, said nothing and got on with the job, even
though his or her personal life was in turmoil. Now, with the
rise of the therapeutic culture, we are more likely to feel sorry
for such people because they cannot express their feelings.
Expressing feelings is held to be desirable because it is believed
to be the way to psychological well-being – and by implication,
psychological well-being is the desired goal of human living. We
also used to admire those who sacrificed their own well-being
and happiness for the sake of others. This might be the ordinary
sacrifices made by parents, especially mothers, for their children, or the sacrifices made by children, especially daughters,
for their parents. Or it might be examples of extraordinary

sacrifice, such as that made by a Mother Teresa or a soldier risk-
ing his life in war. Now we are more inclined to pity those who
made the sacrifices, and we even question their motives or the
desirability of their examples.

What has happened here is a major shift in Western culture,
away from the Christian ethic of duty and sacrifice and self-
denial, and towards a new ethic of the self. This is the therapeutic ethic and sensibility, which says that the most important
goal in life is the well-being of the self.

The culture of emotionalism and religion

Is this cultural shift necessarily anti-Christian or anti-religious?
It often is anti-Christian by implication. For instance, a core
doctrine of the therapeutic culture is that large numbers of us
are ill-fitted to express our feelings or deal with the transitions
in human life because we are emotionally under-developed – we
have an 'emotional deficit' – or, worse, we respond in emotionally inappropriate ways. The Christian legacy is often quite
explicitly blamed for this. For example, Protestant cultures are
condemned for teaching people not to show emotion at all. The
Protestant English are unable to deal with life's crises because
they 'bottle everything up'. Roman Catholic cultures or subcul-
tures are denounced for their heavy emphasis on sin with the
concomitant emotion of guilt. Many of the woes of Irish Roman
Catholics or ex-Roman Catholics are attributed now to this
inheritance.

But behind this is the more fundamental antagonism. Christianity in all its varieties is to be condemned because it creates
and values dependent relationships: it speaks of human beings
as 'children of God'; it commends the dependent love of husband and wife, parent and child. It is within these relationships
that the worst kind of psychological damage is done. This is
why so many popular books are being written with such titles
as 'Women who love too much' or 'When parents love too
much'. There are even 'For people who love their cats too
much' and 'How to be your own best friend'.[10] For this reason

Christian ethics are seen as fundamentally flawed: they invite dependant relationships as people are taught all the time to put the interests of someone else – God, other people – before their own emotional needs.

The remedy is to reject these false guides and to follow paths set out by the new gurus of the various therapeutic remedies. While these remedies are very many and various, what they have in common is an emphasis on feelings and emotions and the conviction that the way to happiness is through psychological health. That psychological health begins with understanding one's own emotions and putting one's own emotional well-being first. Christianity is condemned precisely because it does not commend a turn to the self but a turn from the self – to God and to others. This, it is claimed, leads to all manner of psychological problems as individuals neglect their own emotional well-being and are exploited and abused by the Church, by religion, by other people.

Although I think much of this cultural shift is undesirable and deeply antagonistic to Christianity, I do recognize that there have been valuable insights and I am not advocating the dismantling of counselling services. While many of the theories of counselling seem to me to be very dubious, experienced counsellors clearly can help people in distress, not least because a problem shared is a problem halved – perhaps even principally because it is often helpful to talk. What Christians have to work at is distinguishing what is of value from what, in fact, leads people to make wrong turnings. For instance, there is a danger of pathologizing many ordinary experiences. It is unpleasant to be made redundant, or to fail a job interview, or to lose a partner; but it is not the end of the world. The language of emotional deficit turns an expanding range of life's ordinary experiences into sites of emotional trauma. Over time it fosters a climate in which people feel unable to cope with the ordinary business of living. 'I will survive' – the popular song – reflects this constant emotional struggle. The danger then is that the will to make something of oneself and one's life – self-improvement – is sapped. Christians will also want to repudiate the suggestion that it is always wrong to be self-sacrificial, or always damaging to feel guilty about sins committed. At the same time, we need to understand that there has been a turn to the self, and if Christianity has nothing helpful to say about that, it will fall on deaf ears in a therapeutic culture. Ministry is offered against the backcloth of this therapeutic culture. (See Table 2 for the differences between Christianity and the therapeutic culture.)

Table 2: The human condition according to Christianity and the therapeutic culture

	Christianity	*Therapeutic culture*
The person	Made in the image of God but morally flawed	Self-made but emotionally vulnerable
The human task	Sanctification	Survival
The problem	Sin	Emotional vulnerability
The answer	Grace	Affirmation
Spiritual stance	Turn to God	Turn to self
Expertise	Clergy	Therapists/counsellors
The means	Sacraments/Scripture	Self-knowledge/counselling
Way of life	Obedience to moral law	Follow chosen values
Ultimate goal	Salvation	Emotional well-being

The ministry of the Church

The ministry of the whole Church

I have suggested that ministry is about making real for people the grace of God at particular moments in their (increasingly secular) lives, especially times of significant change or turmoil. In the contemporary Church, ministry is also increasingly understood as the task of the whole people of God, lay and ordained. Although this is taken for granted now, it is a relatively new insight, or, some would say, the recovery of a more biblical understanding of ministry. At any rate, it has become one of the distinguishing marks of the Church in the later twentieth century. A good summary of the shift in emphasis can be found in the Charge that the Methodist Church of Singapore lays before those who are about to be ordained presbyter. The Charge articulates very well this contemporary understanding of ministry and of the respective roles of the lay and the ordained that follow from it. It says:[11]

> We are not ordaining you to ministry; that happened at your baptism.

> We are not ordaining you to be a caring person; you are already called to that.

> We are not ordaining you to serve the Church in committees, activities, organizations; that is already implied in your membership.

> We are not ordaining you to become involved in social issues, ecology, race, politics, revolution, for that is laid upon every Christian.

> We are ordaining you to something smaller and less spectacular: to read and interpret those sacred stories of our community, so that they speak a word to people today; to remember and practise those rituals and rites of meaning that in their poetry address people at the level where change operates; to foster in community through word and sacrament that encounter with truth which will set men and women free to minister as the body of Christ.

> We are ordaining you to the ministry of the word and sacraments and pastoral care.

> God grant you grace not to betray but uphold it, not to deny but affirm it, through Jesus Christ our Lord.

Ministry here is understood as a partnership between lay and ordained, and the role of the ordained is focused on equipping lay people for their ministry. There are three aspects to that, as the Charge says.

First, clergy are to be ministers of the Word. The Christian understanding of the Scriptures is that while Jesus Christ is the Word of God made flesh, the record of his ministry among us are the words of the sacred text. Jesus is the primary Word of God, the New Testament is the word of God in this secondary sense: it is the intermediary for God's Word, the record of his becoming visible, of his fleshly presence with us. If we want to know about Jesus we must first look there, in the Scriptures. In Luther's striking phrase, the New Testament is the manger in which Christ is laid. So we come to the manger. The task for the ordained person is to be immersed in the sacred text, to seek to understand it, and to share that understanding with others, beginning with the Christian community, though not ending there. In the past the minister could assume that the people he came across would have some knowledge and understanding of the Scriptures – but not any longer. When the Bible is read – at one of the occasional offices, for example – it may need some careful introduction. When it is expounded to the congregation, it needs to be done in ways that speak with some clarity about how the Scriptures bear on contemporary living. Increasingly in preaching and teaching we are not just expounding a text but showing how texts help us to reflect on experience or how they challenge us.

In the second place, the clergy celebrate the sacraments. I particularly like the reference to rituals and rites of meaning that 'in their poetry address people at the level where change operates'. The sacraments are able to change people, setting the sinner free of guilt and filling the downcast with hope. We observe this Sunday by Sunday as the congregation comes forward to receive the sacrament. Every parish priest knows how important that moment is for each individual worshipper. There can be tears in someone's eyes or a smile of bliss or a look of relief in the midst of pain. We are all witnesses to the grace of God, healing and encouraging as we break bread and bless wine.

Third, the primary function of the ordained person today is to build up the Christian community so that its members may minister the grace of God to everyone they encounter in the circumstances of their daily lives.

But because ordained ministers are also the visible representatives of the Christian community they are also called upon by those who are not members of the Church. When this happens in today's more secular culture, it is a matter of some significance.

When ministry is sought

In the past, as we have seen, the ordained person performed a range of pastoral functions. However, over the last 150 years most of those have been handed over to, or claimed by, other professionals. Some of those who work in these professions – as teachers, counsellors, welfare workers, probation officers, community workers – are themselves members of churches for whom this is their vocation. The ministry of the ordained is now asked for by those who are not members principally in the context of crises and transitions in people's lives. It is often about the management of change.

The Greek philosopher, Heraclitus, said that we cannot step into the same river twice. Change is an inescapable feature of living. Change is both external to us and internal, and the external change has an impact on us internally: we are affected by our environment. At the level of society and culture there often seems to be a bewildering flux, perhaps more so in modern life than ever before. But even at the level of the individual we are subject to constant change. Some of it we can predict because it is a normal part of growing up and growing old – we pass through stages of development. But much is unforeseen – we fall in love, we fall out of love, we become ill, we are bereaved.

Change may be welcome or unwelcome. We were probably glad to leave adolescence behind and become adult. We look forward to getting married and having a family. But we do not welcome the letter of redundancy, or the diagnosis of cancer, or the loss of our life's partner, or the onset of old age. But all change disorientates. Perhaps that is why the hymn 'Abide with me' is so popular: it acknowledges that change is an inescapable feature of human lives, particularly the change associated with ageing, but suggests that there may be something unchanging, some rock, something of solidity and permanence, that we can cling to – religion!

> Change and decay in all around I see,
> O Thou who changest not,
> Abide with me.

The text may be, 'God is not subject to change', but the subtext is surely, 'My understanding and experience of God, my religion, is not subject to change'. That, of course, is an illusion. The task of the minister is to help people distinguish between the unchanging God and everything else – which is subject to change.

Whether welcome or unwelcome, change is inescapable, and it needs to be managed by us. We manage it in a number of ways but there are two in particular through which religion contributes – story and ritual.

Managing change through story

In the first place, we need some narrative or story that enables us to make sense of change and also to give the changes that happen to us as individuals some significance by allowing them to be seen as part of a larger canvas. We can understand the need for this when we observe what happens in families. Quite often when I visit families to arrange weddings, baptisms or funerals, a photograph album is produced. As the pages are turned it becomes clear what is happening: the story of this family is being told through a series of pictures of key moments in the life of the family. Weddings, births, holidays, family get-togethers, graduations, anniversaries and so on are recalled and their meaning and significance discussed. As the story unfolds, the latest event is incorporated into the on-going narrative. In this way, by taking its place in the wider narrative, it begins to make sense. If we are arranging a wedding, the new member of the family – the son-in-law or daughter-in-law to be – is inducted into the family history and incorporated into the family itself: their story now becomes a strand in the larger story. If it is a funeral, the life of the deceased is given some sort of perspective. What is true at the level of the family is true at other levels too – we need the bigger story into which our individual story can be fitted.

For most Europeans, the Christian narrative of creation–redemption–consummation has performed this function in the past. Each individual human life was understood in the context of God's plan for the whole world. This was the big narrative. We could then begin to give some meaning to our individual lives by reference to that big story. So, for example, if life went well, we could speak of God's blessings but also of our need to show the same kindness and generosity to others that God had shown to us. If life went badly, we might reflect on whether we had forsaken God's plan for us in some way, or, if the cause of our unhappiness lay beyond our power to affect, we would reflect on the resources God had for us to overcome hardships and come through. At all times we would keep before us the vision of the end-point, the coming of God's kingdom of righteousness and peace.

The big narrative runs through the Bible from Genesis to Revelation. There would have been a time when every child in this country learnt the story, in school if not Sunday School or church. However, the content of religious teaching in schools was refashioned significantly from the mid-1960s and the Bible was the principal casualty. The evolving name of the subject reflects the changes: Scripture, Religious Knowledge, Religious Education, Religious Studies.

Today, Christian congregations, though less biblically literate than their forebears, hear the story in every eucharist. It is summed up in each of the eucharistic prayers said over the bread and wine. So, for example, this world is understood as a creation, not a chance or random affair:

You are worthy of our thanks and praise, Lord God of truth,
for by the breath of your mouth you have spoken your word,
and all things have come into being.

This is important. How we think of the world – as intended
or as chance – affects at a deep level how we feel about the
world. From the biblical perspective this is where we were
meant to be. However, this understanding – that God is ultimately responsible for all that is – then raises in us painful questions about his loving purposes in a world of pain.

Human life is likewise regarded as intended, and so significant:

You fashioned us in your image and placed us in the garden
of your delight.

Again, believing that human lives are intended makes a difference to the way we think and feel about human life – though
seeing some people born who are unable to reason or relate
raises those same questions about God's loving purposes.

Even though human beings did not live up to their vocation
to be God's good stewards, they were not abandoned. God continued to seek and to save:

Though we chose the path of rebellion you would not abandon your own. Again and again you drew us into your
covenant of grace.

In the fullness of time, God intervened directly in his creation
in a decisive act of redemption:

Embracing our humanity, Jesus showed us the way of salvation; loving us to the end, he gave himself to death for us.

Death could not contain Jesus, and it will not swallow us up
either. The Holy Spirit will be poured out on Christian people

and one day the entire universe will be restored: there will be a new creation 'brought to perfection in Jesus Christ our Lord'.

This was the narrative that every previous generation of people in this country had heard from their infancy. Each made this big narrative their own: life's experiences and our own reflection on them lead us to value or emphasize some parts of the bigger story more than others. But in the light of that bigger story, individual lives were given shape and meaning.

We manage change, then, first of all by learning the big story – God's creation and redemption of the world and its final consummation – and then slotting our individual stories into it.

This raises the question of how people are inducted into the story in a time of no religion. We can assume that there is little formal teaching in the home, and less than there once was in the school. But little and less is not none at all: cultural Christianity has left its legacy. Parents with young children may pass on an outline of the Christian story or part of the Christian story at key moments of the Christian calendar, especially Christmas and Easter. The content of religious education may be poor, but there is often a real effort made to celebrate the major festivals of the main faiths, particularly Christianity. The culture more generally still acknowledges Christian festivals and symbols. But this presents the churches with a challenge: how do we continue to make known and understood the symbols and stories of Christianity among a less churchgoing population. If local churches could think about evangelism in this way, rather than always wanting their evangelism to result directly in more people in the pews, some interesting and worthwhile projects might be attempted. Here are a few examples of what might be done:

- A church might 'commission' some 'stations of the nativity' from a local primary school, exhibiting them in the church during Advent and inviting the schools to visit.
- Church musicians, actors and writers might put together a musical version of the Easter story and present it in a local park or in a residential home or community centre.

- Several local churches could sponsor a study day on 'death and bereavement' for nurses, doctors, bereavement counsellors and so on, with good professional speakers, including a presentation on the Christian understanding of death and of a 'good death'.

The aim would be to communicate and inform, not to evangelize in the sense of seeking to make people members of the Church.

Managing change through ritual

In the second place, we often also need ritual and ceremony to enable us to move from one period of our life to another or to manage some crisis in our lives or the life of the wider community. In the past, the Christian Church has supplied many of the rituals that mark these moments of transition – rites of passage. Ritual works in a number of ways and at a number of levels. Rituals combine actions, gestures and words. These do several things.

First of all, ritual is a way of managing feeling and emotion. Rituals enable us to express or release or focus feelings. The giving of a ring in the marriage service is a gesture and an action that expresses love. Sometimes rituals have a cathartic or therapeutic effect. Scattering a handful of earth on a coffin or laying a wreath express sorrow and sadness, which can have a soothing and calming effect on a grieving person. Ritual often succeeds where words alone would be considered inadequate or even impossible. 'No words could express what I was feeling,' people will say. Lighting a candle, for example, succeeds in expressing and dealing with the emotions of someone in the shock of bereavement.

But ritual is not just about feeling. Rituals also communicate. They express a point of view. The rituals of the wedding service, for instance, communicate ideas about the ideals of married life and what is necessary to sustain it. This is why the couple enter the church separately – they come from different families

– but leave together – they are now a new family unit. They make their vows in the presence of both sets of families and friends because both have an ongoing role in supporting them in their life together, a role that is often more formally acknowledged in modern rites, such as in *Common Worship*. Rituals affect our perceptions of the world.

Rituals do not simply communicate or allow for the expression or channelling of feeling, they also bring something about: they are events. Take, for example, the rituals by which people become members of professional or occupational groups. There are passing-out parades, the swearing in of judges and magistrates, ordinations, to take a few examples at random. Each ceremony achieves something; it is something done. Because rituals are events, once done they are not easily forgotten. For this reason, we can speak of the wedding ceremony as both something that brings about a changed status and also as something that goes on upholding the marriage.

Change, then, is managed by us through a combination of story and ritual. In the past, the rituals and ceremonies available to people in the management of many of life's most profound and significant changes have been those of the Christian religion. Some of those rituals continue to be called upon by people even if they are not regular attenders at Christian worship. The second part of this book will examine some of these and discuss how they may still speak to people and how the Church might be more sensitive in conducting them. However, whereas in the past the Church had a near-monopoly of these occasions for the management of significant change, this is no longer the case. The therapeutic culture offers an alternative understanding of the human condition. Many rituals – such as lighting candles, the use of incense – have been set free from their anchorage in the Christian story or in Christian places of worship.

Conclusion

What I have suggested in the first part of this book is this. The culture of this country is without question more secular than it was, though it is a secular culture that puts a high premium on emotion rather than reason; it is a therapeutic culture. As part of this, we can discern a turn to the self, a turn inward. Nevertheless, the culture is still deeply influenced by the Christian religion, and most people think of themselves as Christian. It makes sense to speak about cultural Christians and cultural Christianity. People may live more secular lives, but they retain sacred hearts. As a result, the pastoral ministry of the Church is about helping people to appropriate that Christian legacy of story and ritual in order to help them to manage change in their lives, lives that are less community-orientated, more mobile, more fragmented and more individualistic. But if that is to be done effectively we must be aware of the secular challenge that comes to us from the contemporary culture of emotionalism.

Part Two

What people want of the Church

The following three chapters examine the three occasional services of baptism, marriage and the funeral. In each case I shall try to say something about how each of them has changed over the past 30 or 40 years – the changing scene – and then consider what people today might be asking for when they turn to the Church for ministry on these occasions. In each case I shall draw on my own experiences in a particular parish and generalize conclusions from them where possible.

~3~

Why people want their babies christened

O father, for this little life
Entrusted from above,
Ere yet he face earth's sin and strife,
We supplicate thy love.
Gilbert White, 1919, 'O father for this little life'

The changing scene

In this chapter I reflect on the reasons why people who are not members of the Christian Church nevertheless bring their children for baptism and why Christians should encourage and rejoice in this. First, we might note how during the second half of the last century, both evangelical and Catholic clergy began to lose patience with infant baptism, though for different reasons. In each case they were responding to church decline and the loss of traditional clergy roles in society. We have already noted how, throughout the twentieth century, the pastoral role of the clergy was progressively diminished as new professions – social workers, community workers, counsellors – appeared to take over pastoral and welfare work in the community. Clergy lost the sense of being socially useful and felt peripheral in their communities. How could social usefulness be recovered?

Clergy attitudes

Evangelical clergy responded to the loss of social usefulness by abandoning any attempt to regain recognition in the wider community and concentrated on what they saw as the core tasks of the ordained ministry – teaching and propagating

Christian faith. They gained their sense of worth from their role within the Christian congregation, not the wider community. In the past, evangelical Anglicans focused on galvanizing the faith of a nominally Christian nation. Now they believed that Britain was ceasing to be even nominally Christian. The contemporary Church was situated in what looked more and more like a primary mission field: its social context had begun to resemble that of the New Testament Church in the alien culture of the Roman Empire. Since British society was no longer supportive of Christian values, they believed, energies had to be poured into evangelism and securing adult conversion and commitment. Once again there was a world of difference between 'the world' and 'the Church'. To become a Christian in a post-Christian culture required a break to be made as you turned your back on an increasingly godless society and centred your life on Christ and his Church.[1] As a result, every pastoral occasion also had to be approached as an occasion for evangelism: ministry was assimilated to mission.

Infant baptism flew in the face of this approach – the need for a radical break with the world. The meaning of adult baptism was clear and unambiguous: the candidate was making a transition from a past way of life – godless, idolatrous or indifferent – to a Christ-centred one. (This is why Paul is able to make powerful links between the life of the person being baptized and the death and resurrection of Christ. In baptism we 'die' to that former – pagan or Jewish – way of life and 'rise' to the new – Christian – way of life. The waters of baptism become the waters of death in which we die and rise with Christ. This theology of baptism and this understanding of the symbol of the water made perfect sense in the cultural context of early Christianity, in which adults were leaving one tribe and going over to another.)

But in infant baptism the candidate was passive. Infant baptism was not about a break at all. In fact, it seemed to say the opposite. Parents and godparents seemed to think of it as an affirmation and celebration of ordinary family life, with the implication that there was an essential continuity between world and Church. Consequently, evangelical clergy became impatient with infant baptism: it was a distraction from the real business of making adult disciples. It might have been appropriate in a time when almost every child being baptized came from the home of a churchgoing family; now it only clouded the issue – the need for a radical break. This led evangelical clergy to insist that baptism had to be understood as the point at which converted adults declared they had broken with 'the world' and its values and were committing themselves to Christ and his values. Some made infant baptism dependent on the conversion of the parents, or at least their participation in a lengthy preparation; others would only offer 'thanksgiving for the birth of a child', reserving baptism for adults.

Those in the more Catholic tradition also lost interest in infant baptism. Some regretted the way the theological links between baptism and confirmation – the preferred term was 'Christian initiation' – and the themes of Easter were lost with the baptism of babies.[2] Others, especially in urban areas, came under the influence of a number of theologies that shifted the focus of interest in the Christian Church from the individual to the community. This was the effect of the secular and liberation theologies from the late 1960s onwards. Pastoral concern had to begin not with the individual but with his or her social context, otherwise, pastoral work would always be dealing with symptoms and never with causes. For some, this meant that they had to engage directly in local politics and political campaigns. For others, it meant that they had to be involved in community work and community development. The net effect was the same: they ceased to concern themselves with the question of individual salvation, which had been the point of infant baptism.

For the past 50 or so years, therefore, infant baptism has been a theological embarrassment for evangelicals, who sought to discourage it, and an irrelevance to Catholics, who carried on baptizing, though without enthusiasm. We need to step back and start again from a different perspective.

A more sociological approach

Something under one-quarter of all the babies born in England today are baptized in the Church of England. This represents a serious decline since the turn of the last century: in 1900 there were 609 baptisms for every 1000 live births. Even as late as 1956 there were 602. But by 1970 this had fallen to 466 and in the last year of the twentieth century there were 211. Even so, this remains one of those rare occasions when large numbers of people continue to seek the ministry of the Church. Despite this, the Church shows little curiosity about why people want this for their children. Perhaps this is why so many books about Christian baptism seem to both lay and ordained Christians to be unsatisfactory: the preoccupation of the Church is with such matters as the theological justification of infant baptism or the shape of the liturgy. There is less interest in what motivates people who have minimal contact with the Church to seek baptism. There may even be resentment or hostility: 'It means nothing to them, they are not churchgoers'. This is a strange attitude. It is strange because with the other pastoral offices the clergy recognize that they have to invest some time patiently trying to understand people's thoughts, feelings and needs. These occasions touch on matters that may go very deep and are hard to articulate. For example, if the funeral service is to be conducted in a way that is helpful, then the minister must seek to answer the question, 'What does the death of this person mean to these mourners?' This is not usually the approach taken with infant baptism, perhaps because the Church calls baptism a sacrament. It may seem reasonable to ask people what they make of a funeral, but sacraments are the Church's business and so only the Church can say what baptism means. Yet if this pastoral office is also to be an occasion of ministry, those who conduct it or play some part in it need to understand what it is that people want from it and what they think they are doing when they present their babies at the font. What is going on here?

Since the Church shows little interest in this question, it is not surprising that there is little we can say with any certainty. There is scope for research. Until that happens we have to make the best guesses we can. What follows is, therefore, my best guess as one who conducts a baptism service for three or four babies every month. In recent years I have taken to asking parents and godparents, in effect, what they think baptism is all about, as opposed to telling them what I think it is all about. This is not an easy conversation to have. Many people are not particularly reflective about the things they do and do not find it easy to express themselves. In any case, clergy tend to inhibit such conversations: people think we want 'religious' answers and so they try to tell us what they think we would like to hear. Nevertheless, with patience and a more indirect approach we can learn something once people begin to talk.

Clergy tend to want to talk about baptism in terms of beliefs and commitment – belief in Christ as Lord and commitment to live as a disciple of his. Both lead on to regular churchgoing. Since such belief and commitment is quite beyond the capacity of a baby, it creates the problem of infant baptism. As the parents have no intention of becoming regular churchgoers, it also creates a problem of integrity: how can we ask parents and godparents to make these promises sincerely if they can only be fulfilled by attending church? We build hypocrisy and feelings of guilt into the occasion from the very start.

But suppose we leave aside for a moment the usual concerns and adopt a more sociological approach to 'what is going on here?' In *The Elementary Forms of Religious Life*, Emile Durkheim speaks about religious practices such as baptism in terms of 'compulsions which order society'. If this is our starting-point, rather than the traditional concerns of the Church, we may discover fresh ways of looking at this particular pastoral office and be able to offer people genuine ministry.

What do people want from baptism? I will suggest a number of areas of interest, remembering that these observations arise out of a particular context. The social context of each parish church will be different and we need to be sensitive to the context if we are to make sense of what people are asking for. In asking what people want from baptism, we are asking what these particular people in this particular place want. Let me now suggest a number of factors that motivate the people of my parish, St George's, Kendal.

Why do people seek baptism for their children? First of all, we need to rule out, or at least cast some doubt on, some possible reasons.

Social pressures and superstitions

It is sometimes said that people seek baptism for their children as a result of social pressures or because of superstitions. As far as social or family pressures are concerned, if they exist today they are very different from what was sometimes the case in the past. It is rare today to find young people coming for baptism simply to satisfy the wishes of parents or grandparents. There seems little or no expectation one way or another among different age groups in any of the social groups in my parish – working-class and lower-middle-class – that children should be baptized. I would hazard a guess that the same is broadly true across the social spectrum. It is probably going too far to say that there is an opposite expectation. Indifference rather than hostility is the attitude of most people towards religion in Britain today. Occasionally, young mothers complain that their partner has experienced some mocking from his circle of friends – 'Have you got religion now?' – but this is overcome by suggesting that the baptism is something that the women want and the men have to go along with, and such an explanation satisfies. On the whole, if a couple who do not already attend church choose to have their baby baptized, while some members of the family and some friends may privately and momentarily wonder why, they will still gladly accept an invitation to the ceremony and consent to be godparents. Indeed, most people are very flattered and pleased to be asked.

Likewise, most of the superstitions that once surrounded baptism and the now unasked-for practice of 'churching of women' are also largely a thing of the past. When I began my ministry as a parish priest in the 1970s churching in the Book of Common Prayer – The Thanksgiving of Women after Child-birth, commonly called The Churching of Women – was rare but not unknown. There were a few women who would not leave the home until they had been to church to give thanks for a safe deliverance 'from the great pain and peril of Child-birth'. The decline of child mortality has led to these superstitions withering away. Occasionally, parents will now say, shyly, that baptism is an insurance against life's tragedies – rather as you might touch wood or a rabbit's foot. But this is not a common view.

Few now suppose that their children's health or even their eternal salvation is dependent on baptism. Fear of hell is no longer a factor. There would have been a time within living memory when this was a real anxiety. The provision of emergency baptism bears witness to this, though the rubric in *Common Worship* now makes it clear that 'questions of ultimate salvation or of the provision of a Christian funeral for an infant who dies do not depend upon whether or not a child has been baptized.' As late as the early 1970s I was still called upon from time to time to go to a local maternity hospital to baptize infants who were very ill or about to undergo emergency surgery – a reflection of this understanding of baptism.

None of these older practices ought to surprise us. For 400 years the vast majority of children born in this country were baptized according to the Book of Common Prayer, in which the opening words of the service for the Publick Baptism of Infants make the position only too clear:

> None can enter into the kingdom of God, except he be regenerate and born anew of Water and of the Holy Ghost.

The first prayer offered to God says explicitly that baptism, which consists of washing and sanctifying, is the means of avoiding the 'wrath' of God. The opening rubric of the Order for the Burial of the Dead in the same book is equally explicit:

Here is to be noted, that the Office ensuing is not to be used for any that die unbaptized, or excommunicate, or have laid violent hands upon themselves.

These were important issues in a world where the question of eternal salvation was a real concern and where many children died in infancy. In this situation parents needed reassurance, and the Prayer Book went to some lengths in providing it, as long as the child was brought to the font. The portion of Scripture appointed to be read at the baptism was the passage from St Mark's Gospel that spoke of Jesus rebuking his disciples for trying to keep children from him, and then saying, 'Suffer the little children to come unto me, and forbid them not; for of such is the kingdom of God.' The exhortation that followed re-inforced the point and went on:

Doubt ye not therefore, but earnestly believe, that he will likewise favourably receive this present Infant; that he will embrace him with the arms of his mercy; that he will give unto him the blessing of eternal life, and make him partaker of his everlasting kingdom.

Until relatively recently, then, parents in this country have been schooled to want their children to go to heaven if they died and to believe that this depended on being baptized. Few think in these terms now. British society is no longer as saturated with Christian presuppositions as it once was. The context in which the rites of the Church are performed has changed dramatically in something under a century. If people seek baptism for their children today they do so in a culture that has largely lost its hold on traditional Christianity. Inevitably, therefore, infant baptism has changed its meaning.

Four reasons for infant baptism

If we are to discover why people who are not members of the Church nevertheless continue to ask for baptism we need to begin positively, wanting to understand and support them in what it is that they are seeking from the Church, recognizing that they are cultural Christians. As I talk to families, four reasons for baptism become apparent. It is not how the Church normally thinks about baptism.

1. An epiphany – with gifts

Sometimes we miss the significance of the obvious. The obvious point about infant baptism is that it is a 'showing' of a newly born child to a wider circle of family and friends. There is something universal and perhaps quite primaeval about showing a newborn child to visitors who in turn offer gifts – as the children's fairy story 'The Sleeping Beauty' in its many variations suggests. Parents want to show (or show off) their new baby and to share their joy that a child has come into the world with those who play a significant role in their lives. The theological word for showing is 'epiphany' and it is perhaps a pity that the epiphany Gospel is not routinely read at a baptism. That might help us to think more carefully about the significance of specifically *infant* baptism, and infant baptism for those who do not attend church regularly. Like the wise men journeying to visit the holy child, the guests at a baptism come to visit the baby who is shown to them, to express their love and to give gifts.

There is a recognition here that if a child is to grow up and flourish, gifts are needed that others have some power to bestow or withhold. What are the gifts that are brought for the child? Guests bring material presents; but they are only the symbols of the real gifts desired at baptism, which are not material. Those who bring children to a church for their showing are saying that human beings do not live by bread alone. Yes, they will want their child to have everything that their money will allow them to buy. They will want to provide a roof over their child's head, a pleasant home environment, food to eat and clothes to wear. Eventually they will want their child to have a good education and a satisfying job in a peaceful world. But they also know that non-material gifts are as important as material for fulfilled lives. They want their child to grow up blessed with a supportive family and good friends. They also want their child to develop a certain sort of character, to be possessed of particular virtues. This will not happen automatically, simply as a result of being born. The gifts of character will be conferred as a result of the child being raised in and shaped by a particular moral tradition. The infant needs to be – so to speak – born again into that tradition. Parents bring their child to baptism because they understand the truth of this, and they know the Church understands the truth of this. At a baptism the fact that a child's character is not so much innate as formed is acknowledged.

Sometimes one of the partners has not thought this through particularly well. One man said at a preparation class, 'If it was left to me, we wouldn't be here. I think he should be allowed to grow up and make decisions for himself about what he thinks, and right and wrong, when he's older, a teenager.' Women are usually much clearer about the need to bring up children according to a set of consistent principles, for no child can be raised in a moral vacuum. Those who bring children for baptism know that their children are open to all manner of influences from the moment they are born. Parents, therefore, need to ensure, as far as they can, that their children are influenced by the moral values they think are good and worthwhile. This is one of the points of overlap between the traditional concerns of the Church and those of the contemporary parent. Some of the best discussions I have with parents and godparents are around the question of character. The virtues which the families believe are important and want to see cultivated in their children are understood as those of Jesus or of Christianity. This is why they come to church. If asked, parents will explain them. At a recent class the parents and godparents offered these: love, respect for other people, caring for your family and friends, helping other people, making something of your life, and 'trying to leave the world a bit better than how you found it'. All of these, they said, were what Jesus taught us. The role of the minister is to help families articulate this more fluently, making explicit links between what they are feeling for and the baptismal affirmations: 'I turn to Christ', 'I submit to Christ', 'I come to Christ'.

Parents who come for Christian baptism also realize that these virtues have to be struggled for and may not easily be won – you need all the help you can get, including spiritual help. This is why the question in the Book of Common Prayer baptism service had such force:

> Dost thou in the name of this Child, renounce the devil and all his works, the vain pomp and glory of this world, with all covetous desires of the same, and the carnal desires of the flesh, so that thou wilt not follow nor be led by them?

That has been replaced in *Common Worship* with the three questions: Do you reject the devil and all rebellion against God? Do you renounce the deceit and corruption of evil? Do you repent of the sins that separate us from God and neighbour? The language does not resonate in quite the same way and the struggle does not seem quite as titanic.

But whatever form of service is used, there is opportunity for the baptizing priest to explain some fundamental Christian doctrine about the 'fallen' nature of our human condition, which each newborn child will share. One easily understood way of speaking about original sin is to speak of original self-centredness. Every parent will understand that a baby is the centre of its own world – and has to be to survive. It demands food, nappy-changing and attention, and it squawks until it gets what it wants. Growing up is learning that there are other people in the world who also have needs and whose needs may sometimes count for more than one's own. We cannot stay babies all our lives! Since children learn by observing the behaviour of those around them,

the most powerful antidote to self-centredness is the example of
unselfishness in those whom they love and trust – their parents.
Teaching children by example not to be self-centred is a challenge
to each set of parents. The Christian sacraments symbolize the
need for grace – God's help, spiritual help – if we are to fight the
good fight. (Many of these sentiments run counter to the therapeutic sensibility of the times.)

I once asked a group of churchgoing young mothers to com-
pose a prayer that could be said at the baptism of one of their
children, in light of the question, 'What are you hoping for in
seeking baptism?' They looked at prayers in the Church's own
liturgies and at books of prayers and then wrote this:

> Heavenly Father, thank you for [Jack], whom you have given
> to us to love and care for. May your loving arms surround
> him today and every day of his life. Bless his eyes and show
> him the beauty of your world. Bless his ears and teach him to
> hear what is good. Bless his mouth that he may learn to laugh
> and to speak. Bless his feet and guide him along the right
> road. Thank you for his parents, [Janet and John]. Help them
> to bring him up well, knowing right from wrong and good
> from evil. Help us all to surround him with love so that he
> may become loving too. May we never do anything to cause
> him to stumble, and give him a peaceful world to grow up in.
> We make our prayer through Jesus, who blessed the little chil-
> dren. Amen.

The mothers were churchgoers but I am sure the sentiments
they expressed would resonate with most of the families that
seek baptism.

2. Rite of passage for parents

In the second place, baptism is a rite of passage – for the parents!

During the course of the past 10–15 years there have been
two striking developments among those seeking infant baptism

in St George's parish: the parents are less likely to be married and, while the overall number of baptisms may have fallen, the numbers attending have increased. The two phenomena are related. We need to think about what this means.

Where parents are not married, baptism offers the couple the first opportunity to celebrate with family and friends not just the arrival of their child but also their partnership. Weddings are very expensive occasions – special clothes, limousines, flowers, a reception in a hotel, a honeymoon. One can quite see why weddings get put off. In addition, others expect to be either involved in the planning of them – principally the parents of the couple – or placated if they are not. But a baptism is the responsibility of the baby's parents alone. A baptism party allows a couple to gather around them the significant people in their life for what may be their first major celebration as a couple. For some, now, baptism has replaced the wedding as the couple's public acknowledgement of their commitment to each other, and the baptism party has replaced the wedding reception. Some baptism parties begin with afternoon tea and end with a disco, exactly like a wedding.

Second, whether the couple are unmarried or married, the baptism also marks a significant development in their relationship. In traditional societies the decision to have children was inseparable from the decision to marry. But with the appearance in the 1960s of reliable contraceptives that women could control, the decision to have a child was a separate decision, taken on another occasion. It marks a significant turning point in a couple's relationship. Until the birth of this child either partner could walk away from the other and feel under no compulsion to look back, even if married. Now, whatever happens between the partners, they are related, not by marriage but by a blood relationship – the child they have brought into the world together. Marriages can be set aside; but this man and this woman will always be this child's biological parents. That can never be set aside. A baptism in the context of contemporary patterns of living is first of all an occasion of great significance for the couple's own relationship. It marks a considerable change of gear. For some very young people it is like a coming of age. For all it is an unambiguous joining of the settled world of older generations with their particular patterns and rhythms of living.

The baptism of a child signals for all couples, whether married or not, and in a way that the birth alone does not, that they are now prepared to adjust to a different sort of relationship. They are saying that they are ready to settle to the demanding task of raising a family and playing a full part in what that will require. Having a child may bring great joy and satisfaction but it also brings considerable responsibility. This means finding a new centre to their life together, one that includes a third party and one that takes greater note of the surrounding community. The time, affection, loyalty and love that the one partner had exclusively for the other are now to be shared with a third person, a third person who will be very demanding for very many years to come. It also means that they are ready to engage with the wider community. They know that having a child is going to mean involvement with surgeries and clinics, playgroups and nurseries, and ultimately with all the groups and societies that children want to belong to. The centre of gravity of life will now begin to move – from the pubs and clubs of the partners, to the interests of the growing child. In this parish, this involves a mental shift from the town centre to the more immediate neighbourhood – the local shops and schools. The birth of a child commits a couple to their locality in potentially new and more intensive ways. All this is being acknowledged publicly at a baptism. This may not be articulated, but it is understood. Men and women know what baptism means. A baptism is a rite of passage for them, the parents.

3. Women take control

A third factor to note about baptisms is that, in this parish, they are arranged by women. Occasionally the man takes the initiative, but this is rare. Even if he appears at the vicarage to collect an application form it is usually because 'the wife sent me'. In preparation classes, men will often contrive to look bored or uninterested. After the service, young men in particular rush for the door. This partly reflects the fact that in many working-class and lower-middle-class households most of the decision-making to do with the home or the family is still left to the women, despite three decades of talk about shared marital responsibilities. But it also reflects the fact that baptism is an occasion of greater significance for women. This is because a baptism represents an opportunity for the woman to get her partner to do something which many men are reluctant to do: think about the changed relationship that having a child brings. One woman expressed it like this: 'Usually I can never get him to be serious about us as a family. He never sits long enough to have a proper talk about us and the future. He has his tea and then just wants to watch television or go out with his mates. But he had to talk about godparents and everything.' This is not unusual. Working-class men still seem only too happy to leave to their partner as much of domestic life as they can reasonably get away with. But if a baptism is to be arranged, they have to sit down and talk about it, and that offers the chance of a serious conversation about 'us as a family'. Arranging a baptism is one way in which women assert themselves and take some control over their domestic situation. It is one way in which they get men to commit themselves. A baptism helps women to bind men more tightly into family life.

We often observe the men struggling with this. At the end of the service the men and boys leave the church quickly. They hang around outside smoking and talking loudly. The women linger in the church, talk to the parents and admire the baby's baptism outfit. The father of the baby and the male godparents are also required to remain for family photographs, but they often stand about uncomfortably, anxious to join their male friends outside.

There are some people (again, usually women) for whom a baptism has another significance. One woman spoke very movingly of the hard time she had as a child in a dysfunctional family. She said that she didn't want her child to suffer in the same way and that coming to baptism marked her determination 'to see he had a better start in life than I did'. Similarly, for single parents this is an occasion when they can assert their normality and respectability. 'I was determined to have him christened. I want him to have the best. I'm as good as them,' I heard one single mother say to her friend, nodding towards two other families that had come to the preparation class. The baptism of a child is something that respectable families do, so for this mother it was her way of saying, 'I may be on my own but I can still be a proper mother to him. I can be respectable.'

Baptism is a sacrament of radical equality: all may be baptized. Becoming a child of God by adoption and grace is a gift that can be bestowed on anyone, whatever his or her social class, race or sex, because in God's eyes these differences are not significant. (This was why baptism was so important in the first days of the Church, when congregations consisted of people who were socially and economically unequal – slave and free, Greek and Jew, man and woman. How were they to treat one another within the congregation? The answer was: as equals, because they were all equally baptized Christians. This continues to be important for those who are nervous about their social standing and so their child's social standing.) One teenage single mother explained this to me in this way: 'I made a bad mistake and I'm paying for it. But she's done nothing wrong. I want her to have as good a start as the others. God don't hold it against her, what I did.' Baptism was one way in which she signalled to herself, her family and the community this determination to give her daughter a good start.

This is one reason why the symbolism in the baptism service is effective. The priest takes the child in his arms and washes him or her. The way the child is held is evocative of bath-time. Just as the child is washed physically clean at bath-time, so here he or she will be washed spiritually clean: he or she will be made spiritually fragrant and ready to face the future.

4. Acknowledgement of community and rejection of radical individualism

Finally – and returning to the obvious – a baptism at St George's is a public occasion. There are usually at least two children to be baptized at every service and each child brings not less than 20 and often as many as 60 or more members of the family and friends. Quite often members of one baptism group recognize friends in other parties. The conversations before and after the service are frequently drawn out and animated. But in any case, even if there is only one baptism party, a christening symbolizes the inter-relatedness of the human family and the fact that every child born into the world needs that wider human family if it is to flourish.

Baptism is an important symbol of the rejection of the more radical individualism of the times. The people here are acknowledging through their choice of godparents and the presence of the rest of the congregation that this child is part of a bigger family – the human family. It is a visible symbol of the fact that while, in many respects, we do live more private, individual, atomized lives, this does not mean that the community can be dispensed with or that the sense of community has been entirely lost. A baptism service is one of the places where the concern we have for our neighbours in the community and our interconnectedness is made visible.

There is a point in the service where this is made very apparent. At the moment of baptism, the parents do something of great significance: they hand their child over to the baptizing priest. The priest represents, yes, the Christian faith and the Christian community, but also the human community. This handing over is a recognition that each child born into the world is not only a member of his or her own family but the Christian family and the wider human family as well. The symbolism is powerful, though, as with all symbolism, it works its way in us at a subliminal level.

Conclusion

We can jump to the conclusion too quickly that those who bring children for baptism with no intention of becoming regular churchgoers are only looking for an excuse for a party. If this were the case, there is nothing to stop the parents simply holding a secular celebration, a naming ceremony without a baptism, as some do. If people seek a baptism as well as a party at the birth of their child this is significant.

But, awkwardly, people bring their own concerns and needs to a baptism, in the belief that the Church has something to say and something it can do about them. Their concern is not with baptism as a rite of initiation into the Christian Church – if by that we mean attending the local church regularly. If that is emphasized, it can only make them feel hypocritical and the clergy uncomfortable. They do want to identify themselves and the child with Jesus Christ – initiation into the fellowship of Christ's religion – though that does not necessarily mean becoming churchgoers. But, as we have seen, their concern is also with showing their baby to a wider circle of family and friends and finding some wisdom and grace to help them as parents. Christian themes about original sin, human interdependence and God's grace are all important for those who bring babies to be christened, if only those themes can be highlighted.

But is baptism not a sacrament and therefore not open to us to determine what it shall or shall not mean? Yes, baptism is a sacrament. Protestants and Catholics agree on that! The reason they agree is because it is one of the two sacraments which it is believed the Lord himself initiated (the other being the eucharist). But whatever the origins of baptism, it remains a symbolic action whose meaning is bound to change as cultural circumstances change. This is not to say that nothing of the original meaning of the sacrament remains, only that we adapt the meaning according to circumstances. In early Christianity, baptism signified a conscious rejection of one religion and its attendant way of life – whether Jewish or pagan – and the adoption of another – Christianity. When Europe became Christian and people were raised as Christians from birth, baptism could hardly mean that at whatever age it was administered, and so the emphasis fell somewhere else. In the Prayer Book, the theological meaning of infant baptism is that by it the child is 'regenerate and born anew', washed clean of original sin and made safe for heaven. But we can also see it as an identification with and an affirmation of the Christian religion in which the child will be nurtured and of the Christian way of life. This is why the Gospel reading in the Prayer Book is so appropriate – Jesus rebuking the disciples for trying to stop children being brought to him (Mark 10.13f). In the changed circumstances of contemporary life, infant baptism allows parents to give public expression to some deeply held convictions about the purpose and value of human life as Christianity sees it and to make some important commitments to the upbringing of their child.

What I have said suggests that there is a continuity between world and Church and only those who accept that basic stance will be comfortable with infant baptism. This will not be acceptable to those who now want to take the Church in a different direction by assimilating ministry to mission and emphasizing the need for a radical break. The price we pay is that we lose contact with a large proportion of the non-churchgoing but Christian population at this crucial moment in their lives – the birth of a child – and fail to nourish and educate their faith.

But there is a connection between baptism understood in this way and mission. What is being displayed at every baptism is the relevance of Christian faith to mundane concerns, such as the successful raising of children. Infant baptism is one of those increasingly rare occasions when Christians can demonstrate that they do not think of themselves – in Bonhoeffer's striking image – as travelling in a sealed train through enemy territory.

4

Why people get married in church

But could youth last, and love still breed,
Had joys no date, nor age no need,
Then these delights my mind might move
To live with thee and be thy Love.
Sir Walter Raleigh, *Her Reply*

The changing scene

Why do people who are not churchgoers want a church wedding? At one time the answer might have been straightforward, for the alternative to the church was a grim-looking register office in a town centre where car parking was difficult and numbers were limited. But today people are spoilt for choice as far as the venue for their wedding is concerned. The question is, then, less straightforward. However, if we are to minister effectively to people when they ask to get married in church we need to be able to puzzle out an answer. In this chapter I first consider how marriage has changed in recent years and then turn more directly to the less straightforward question: why do people who are not regular churchgoers want a church wedding in preference to other, secular possibilities?

Marriage and Christianity

Baptism is a rite of the Church, but marriage is found in all human societies: it is a human, and not an exclusively Church, institution. Jesus may have 'adorned and beautified with his presence and first miracle' the village wedding at Cana-in-Galilee, but people had been marrying before Christ turned water into wine.[1] As far as we can tell, humanity has had a near-universal concern to raise children within exclusive sexual and affectionate unions of husband and wife. Marriage has been valued throughout human history because it has enabled human beings to flourish. It is certainly not true, as some socialists and feminists have sometimes claimed, that marriage is a bourgeois or capitalist invention.[2] On the contrary, the prayer book is more accurate in describing marriage as a 'gift of God in creation'.

For much of the first Christian millennium, Christians married according to local custom rather than any ceremony of the Church. The Letter to Diognetus from the second century, for example, says that Christians married much as everyone else.[3] What made Christian marriages different was the insistence by the Church on a strict fidelity – especially for men in a patriarchal culture – and a reluctance to sanction divorce. But even as the early Church extended its influence it seems to have taken a long time before it became the major shareholder in weddings, and even longer before it had a monopoly. Although some bishops and theologians urged people to have a ceremony in the church, a full marriage service only makes its appearance in the ninth century. Gradually the setting for a wedding moved from the home to the church.

In this country, from the early Middle Ages, marriage vows were exchanged in the church in front of the priest, and in English. After the Reformation, the Church of England's Book of Common Prayer of 1662 provided a service that remained in use until the alternative forms of the twentieth century. In the eighteenth century, mainly for reasons of property and inheritance, the state began to take a greater interest in marriage, requiring marriages to be publicly registered from 1753 (The Hardwicke Act). Apart from Quakers and Jews, everyone in England was married according to the Anglican rite.[4] The effect of the State's intervention was to give the impression that marriages were made as a result of the marriage ceremony rather than seeing them as being formed over a longer period – courtship, betrothal, ceremony, consummation. When liturgical changes came – there was revision in 1928 and then again after the Second World War – they were because marriage itself had undergone a profound change. This can be described in both sociological and psychological terms. For example, there has been an undoubted emancipation of women, charted by both sociology and psychology, and this has had an impact on the relationship of man and woman in marriage. We can summarize the changes as a move from marriage as a given role in a patriarchal society to marriage as a negotiated role in a more egalitarian one. The successive marriage services of the Church of England mirror these changes. But in whichever century we care to look, marriage had generally been understood as a process rather than a single event. Marriage required some form of betrothal, some public exchange of vows, and then sexual consummation.

Traditional marriage: 'given' roles

What do I mean by marriage as 'a given role' and as a 'negotiated' role?

Martha Nussbaum has suggested that we make sense of our lives by constructing a story about them. We see ourselves rather as we see the characters in a novel playing out a role; what she calls 'fictionalizing' our lives.[5] In the first half of the last century, the story people told about their marriages tended to be one that society had already made familiar. In that story men and women had their respective roles clearly delineated. People still lived in relatively close-knit communities in which lives were lived out with constant reference to the norms of the local community. As far as marriage was concerned, the couple getting married stepped into roles that were already well understood and well defined – whether the couple were happy with that or not. When a man and woman came to see the vicar to arrange a wedding, certain assumptions were made about the role of husband and wife that needed no discussion or explanation: they were 'given'.

The elements of this given role arose originally from the needs of an industrial society that separated home and work. It was assumed, for instance, that a primary purpose of marriage was to create an economically stable household in which children could be born and nurtured. To that end, men were expected to be 'the breadwinners' who would go out to work and support their wife and family. In return, wives would bear the children and look after the home, taking responsibility for cooking and cleaning. In working-class parishes, wives were also responsible for the family finances and for making decisions about the balance between saving and spending. Husbands handed their wage packets over on Friday nights and received back pocket money for beer and cigarettes. The women paid all the bills and saved what they could. Men could have a life of their own outside the marriage provided that they did nothing to destabilize the family. Destabilization was caused by hobbies or interests that took up too much time, or by excessive drinking or womanizing. But roles and rules were clear. Provided that the basic rules were adhered to, any other qualities that a man or woman might bring to the marriage were a bonus and not essential.

I grew up in just such a working-class community in an East Midlands industrial town. These communities had great strengths. They provided a coherent framework within which you could make sense of the world and your place within it. They gave practical support to families in any number of ways, great and small. My mother was able to go out to work because an elderly neighbour allowed my brother and me to come from school each day to her house for tea – which we shared at a kitchen table with her two cats. When elderly widows fell ill, neighbours organized informal rotas for shopping and cleaning and visiting. A death in the street was also a community affair: the layer-out prepared the body, the Dorothy Road Fellowship arranged for a wreath and a collection for the family. In the absence of a developed welfare state these informal arrangements enabled people to survive the vicissitudes of life.

But these communities had a down-side. Each had its unwritten code of permissible behaviour and if you did not conform to it you ran the risk of disapproval. This extended from muttering to stigmatization or even ostracism. Two gay men were tolerated because they did not flaunt their homosexuality, but two lesbian women who did were cold-shouldered and eventually left the neighbourhood. As far as marriage was concerned, the traditional understanding of marriage and the patriarchal household was simply assumed: living together was not an option.[6] This is the nature of the close-knit geographical community and this is what the British people turned their back on in the post-war period – while sometimes remaining nostalgic for a romanticized version of it.[7]

The traditional understanding of marriage was reflected in and shaped by the Book of Common Prayer. By the time I came to conduct weddings in the late 1960s the majority of churches were probably using the 1928 version of the prayer book even though, strictly speaking, this had never been authorized.[8] This softened the rather more robust language of the Solemnization of Matrimony in the Book of Common Prayer. In the 1662 version, the introduction states that marriage should not be 'enterprised, nor taken in hand, unadvisedly, lightly, or wantonly, to satisfy men's carnal lusts and appetites, like brute beasts that have no understanding.' (Luther had said that marriage was a hospital for curing lust.) It goes on to set out the reasons for people marrying in this order: 'for the procreation of children', 'for a remedy against sin, and to avoid fornication' and 'for the mutual society, help and comfort that the one ought to have of the other'. During the course of the twentieth century this order, and the assumption that marriage, sex and children went together, was largely rejected. People no longer believed that the primary purpose of marriage was to have children, and easily available contraceptives made it possible to separate sex from procreation. (This has probably been the single most influential change affecting modern marriage.[9]) Nor did they regard sex before marriage as a sin. (Full employment and reasonable wages made it possible for young people to set up homes of their own.) Living together replaced earlier patterns of courting and 'going steady'. The final reason for marriage – 'mutual society, help and comfort', in a relationship of mutual enrichment and equality – became the most important reason. Or rather, as people increasingly lived together before marriage, the marriage relationship was seen not as something new and quite different from what had been there before, but as an intensification of it. By the beginning of the twenty-first century, 'mutual society, help and comfort' had become the single most important reason for marrying. It was these changes that the Church sought to reflect, as far as traditional teaching permitted, in successive revisions of the marriage service.

Modern marriage: 'negotiated' roles

From the 1960s people began to be more independent of society's norms (which reflected the teaching of the Church as set out in the Prayer Book) and wanted to assert their individuality and autonomy more. As far as intimate relationships were concerned this meant constructing the story of their marriages differently and creating new roles for themselves within marriage. Over the past 50 or so years we have seen a moving away from a familiar story with its given roles – the traditional understanding of marriage – to something that requires couples to *negotiate* more between themselves. As a result, marriage is becoming what one theological commentator has called 'a permanent do-it-yourself project privileging the emotional and inter-personal aspects of the relationship'[10] – a further aspect of the therapeutic culture.

Traditional communities, whether working-class or middle-class, largely collapsed in the period following the Second World War. Patterns of employment changed: men and women no longer spent their whole working lives in the same factory or office. Patterns of living changed: people wanted their home to be away from their place of work. Patterns of leisure changed: social activities did not revolve around the local community. Patterns of welfare changed: informal arrangements gave way to an extended welfare state. Increasingly, people lived in one place, worked in another, and pursued leisure activities over a wide area. Lives became more mobile, more fragmented and more individualistic. A range of new professionals emerged to help people through times of crisis. All of these changes contributed to the breaking down of strong, local communities exercising an influence over how people lived their lives, including their married lives.

We should not exaggerate the scope of the change from given to negotiated roles. It is not true that nothing was previously negotiated, though that was easier to do between the partners within a marriage than it was between them and the wider society. There were always a few people who managed to lead a different way of married life by subtle negotiation. For example, in the street in which I grew up, there was one couple who also had lovers that came and went. They were tolerated because – my mother said it in a whisper – they managed to persuade their neighbours that they were really gypsies and not like everyone else.

But we should not suppose that marriages now are totally negotiated. It is rather that the range of possibilities has been enlarged. Even though it became possible for women outside the home to take jobs and have careers, it was still more probable than not that inside the home domestic roles remained much as they always had. A man might share the cooking, cleaning and childcare, but ultimate responsibility for these matters was still more likely to rest with the woman. This was particularly true among working-class families, less so with professionals. So there are continuities and discontinuities.

These changes are reflected in the different revisions of the marriage service. For example, by 1980, when the Alternative Service Book came into use, the introduction to the marriage service both altered the order of the reasons for marriage and also presented sex (though somewhat coyly) in a far more positive manner:[11]

Marriage is given, that husband and wife may comfort and help each other, living faithfully together in need and in plenty, in sorrow and in joy. It is given that with delight and tenderness they may know each other in love, and, through the joy of their bodily union, may strengthen the union of their hearts and lives. It is given, that they may have children and be blessed in caring for them and bringing them up in accordance with God's will, to his praise and glory.

Common Worship, authorized for use in 2000, reflects further developments. In a Pastoral Introduction – not read as part of the service – it speaks of marriage as a 'creative relationship', which suggests that the couple themselves do not simply step into wholly preconceived roles but have to work things out together. In the service itself, an extended Preface, setting out the reasons for marriage, follows the order of the Alternative Service Book: marriage is given that a man and woman may 'grow together in love and trust', it is about 'sexual union' and it is given as 'the foundation of family life'. But there is a recognition that the couple may already have children. If they do, then the word 'born' is omitted and the priest says that marriage is given as the foundation of family life in which children are 'nurtured.'[12]

But while the Church sought to accommodate some changes in this way, there were limits to what it would say. Not all trends in modern marriage find a sympathetic echo in the marriage service.

Trends in marriage

Of these trends, four are perhaps most significant. First, we ought to note that a growing number of people decide not to get married at all but simply to live together. The number of people getting married has declined continuously and steadily since 1972. This was the peak year, with some 426,241 marriages. By 2001 it had fallen to 249,227. This represents the smallest absolute number of marriages since 1897, despite the fact that the population has increased by some 20 million. For some people, living together is preferred to being married.

They will never be married. Some are beginning to ask for legal recognition of this state of living together but not being married, and the government seems ready to respond. This is already recognized in France, where couples can enter into a *pacte civil de solidarité*, which gives some legal protection but can be annulled quickly if either party so desires.

This does raise the interesting question of when marriage 'happens'. If a marriage is – to use the definition enshrined in English law – 'the voluntary union for life of one man and one woman', then what makes a marriage is the couple's mutual consent. What happens at the wedding ceremony is that this consent is declared, made public, in front of a registrar and witnesses. This is why some people have argued that some forms of cohabitation – where a couple are committed to one another and live together faithfully with every intention of staying together – look very much like a marriage. So why do they not get married?[13]

There may be a number of reasons for opposition to marriage. Some will insist that marriage is 'only a piece of paper' – they already have the committed relationship and no ceremony can add to that. For others, marriage will always carry with it an association with patriarchy – an unequal relationship in which women are the losers. For a few – and this is a more recent development – it is the fact that marriage is 'for better, for worse' that is the problem. They believe this most intimate of relationships between a man and woman has to be sustained by constant attention to the emotional satisfactions each is getting from it. There can never be anything 'taken-for-granted' about it. If it should fail, for one or both, there should be the possibility of walking away without the kind of trauma that generally attends the breakdown of a marriage.

This new sort of relationship – contractual rather than covenantal, and sometimes called the 'pure relationship' – is less easy to defend when there are children.[14] They have needs that crucially depend on the stability and continuity of their parents' relationship. Although the majority of people do not think in terms of such 'pure relationships', enough probably now do to have a more general influence on the way people think about the man–woman relationship.

What all this points to is the fact that relationships between men and women are rather more complex than any simple categorization of 'married' and 'cohabiting' would suggest. For the majority of people, however, living together without marrying is what they do for a while. Eventually they do get married, often when children come along.

A second trend we can discern is that fewer people now marry in church. We have become used to headlines such as this one in the *Independent* newspaper in 2003: 'Weddings fall to Victorian levels as church is shunned'.[15] In 2001, there were 88,989 church weddings, 36 per cent of the total. By 2003, church weddings accounted for only one-quarter of the total. This is a very significant change since 1991 when half of all weddings were conducted in churches, and it reflects the working out of the 1994 Marriage Act, which allowed for weddings in registered buildings that are neither churches nor register offices. (The Anglican Church resisted this trend at first, refusing to allow ministers to be involved. More recently it has begun to change its attitude.) By 2001, one-third of all civil marriages took place in hotels, football stadiums, country clubs and the like. According to an on-line 'wedding event' organizer, the most desirable venues for weddings in 2002 were the London Eye, the Lanesborough Hotel, Epsom Race Course, the Institute of Contemporary Arts, Pennyhill Park and Spa in Surrey, Hanbury Manor Hotel in Hertfordshire, Rowton Castle in Shrewsbury, Brookfield Manor in Derbyshire, Allerton Castle in Leeds and Linthwaite Hall in Cumbria.[16] In 2003, the Church of England became so concerned at this trend that it attempted to market its 16,000 parish churches at National Wedding Shows in Birmingham and Earls Court.

There is also a gathering momentum to change the necessity to have both a registered building as well as a registered person conducting the ceremony and to have a celebrant-based marriage. In other words, people might be able to marry any-where, subject to the agreement of the couple and the cele-brant. If this happens we can expect weddings in all kinds of unusual and bizarre settings, as happens in the USA.

Table 3: How marriage has changed

	1897	2001
Population	32,000,000	52,000,000
Total marriages	249,145	249,227
Church of England weddings	68%	22%
Civil weddings	14%	64%

Data from the Office for National Statistics

Finally, we notice the number of weddings that are second or subsequent marriages. It was not unusual for people in past cen-turies to marry more than once, but in the past marriages were ended by the early death of a partner rather than by divorce. Today, second marriages are more commonly the result of divorce. One reason for the increase in divorce may be because modern negotiated marriage is more demanding than tradi-tional marriage. At any rate, there has been more discontent with marriage, and this has contributed towards the divorce rate soaring, with women generally initiating the proceedings. In 2001, both parties married for the first time in only 60 per cent of marriages. However, there has been one constant: aver-age ages have remained at about 34 for men and 32 for women.

Four reasons for a church wedding

If this is something of the backcloth against which modern mar-riages are entered into, let me now turn to weddings in my parish. No one these days is compelled to get married in order to live with a boyfriend or girlfriend. Moreover, if two people do decide to marry, and they are not regular churchgoers, there are many attractive, secular alternatives to a church wedding, espe-cially near Kendal in the Lake District. We can, therefore, fairly assume that the decision to marry in a church does have a significance that it might not have had when there were social pressures to marry and when a municipal register office was the only alternative. Why then do people get married in St George's Church?

If couples are asked in a direct way why they want to get married in church they search for what they feel is a religiously acceptable answer. This may not be on the tip of the tongue![17] But if an unforced conversation can develop around the subject of their marriage, many interesting things gradually emerge. As I talk to couples, the four reasons set out below seem to me to be the principal reasons for their choice of a church wedding. Some of these reasons lead couples to seek a church wedding, some to seek a church wedding at this particular church, and some lead to a mixture of the two.

1. Rite of passage into a specific community

Let us begin again with the obvious. First, I note that in this parish, as in most parishes, marriage no longer means the beginning of an intimate and sexual phase of a relationship between a man and a woman. All the people I marry now are living together and a few have children. That is the norm for all weddings and has been for some time: the last generation of grandparents who could be shocked by this has probably now passed on. The marriage service of the Church, however, by and large reflects the traditional understanding of marriage as the beginning of an intimate relationship and the precursor to family life, though, as we have seen, there are one or two points where the contemporary reality shows itself. So how does the relationship change when a couple marry and how does marriage in church affect that?

Behind the question is some perplexity: we are not sure how the relationship can change or how the church service can add anything if the couple already live together. Here I think it is helpful to recall Martha Nussbaum's suggestion that we live by fictionalizing our lives. We tell a story about our world and our lives within it. In this way we make sense of who we are and why we do the things we do. When people get married they begin to tell a new story about themselves. If, then, people are already living together, how does marriage cause the story they tell about themselves to change?

What couples say to me is that marriage signifies an acceptance by them that they are now ready to join the ranks of those who are already married. This is, as one young man told me, a 'change of gear'. This 'going up a gear' seemed to refer in the first place to how the couple think of themselves within the wider community. Their sense of self changes: getting married means leaving behind the world of the non-married. The way couples speak about the change is in part captured in the remark of one thoughtful woman, who said: 'We've had to turn ourselves round. I only used to live from weekend to weekend. Now I find myself looking much further forward all the time.' When I asked her to explain, she said that before she didn't feel she and her partner had to think about what might lie in the more distant future – where their jobs were going, whether they would always be able to pay the mortgage, whether they would have enough set aside for pensions, whether they would have provision for children's education. All that had changed, and these were precisely the things that now occupied her mind more and more. This had stolen up on her and meant she was now 'ready for marriage'. The important goals in her life related increasingly to the longer term. She felt she was becoming more like her neighbours, most of whom had been married for some years and had growing families. One man in his early 30s said, 'I always knew we would get married one day. But it scared me. I wanted to put it off as long as I could because I knew that when we got married we would turn into me mam and dad.' He also said it was like leaving adolescence behind. This was good news for his partner, since he was now approaching 30. What he seemed to mean was that once he was married it was expected of him that he would spend less time with his single friends in pubs and clubs and on the terraces on Saturday and would devote more time to wife and home. Marriage involved a significant further withdrawal from those separate mental and physical worlds that unmarried men and women inhabit. All that would now be left would be the occasional girls' or boys' 'night out'.

Marriage alters the relationship not only of the couple themselves but also of their respective families. In this parish, clan relationships, and the loyalties they create, are an important matter. After the wedding, the groom ceases to be simply the daughter's boyfriend or partner; he is now their son-in-law and so more decidedly part of the family and a member of the tribe. Whatever feelings the rest of the family had towards the partner, the ritual of marrying lays upon everyone the obligation to set aside hesitations and doubts and to welcome him or her within the wider family. This is reinforced by a wedding in a particular building because over time particular buildings become associated with particular families. This is especially true of churches, which are used to mark a number of key moments in the life of a family and not just weddings. In Kendal, St George's is the church where certain couple's parents, relatives and friends were married, where they and their children and their friends' children were baptized, and where the funerals of members of their family and their friends have been held. The church still performs the function of a parish church.

The marriage rite is, then, a rite of passage. It moves people on in the way they 'fictionalize' their lives from one way of life – which is much closer to that of single people who live with less reference to the surrounding community, and perhaps live much more for the day – to another – which is much closer to that of one's married parents and older neighbours. In important respects it is a move *into* the community; specifically, into *this* community. For this reason it makes sense to marry at the local church rather than in some remote hotel, however lovely the setting, because this is where important events in the life of this tribe are recorded.

2. Deepening an established relationship

Marriage, then, does not mean the beginning of an intimate, sexual relationship; the two people are already living together. Nor does it necessarily mean the beginning of a family; there may already be children. But it does signify a change within a relationship, however subtle and hard to define. If people have been living together, something happens to make them take a step that involves a considerable amount of planning and expense, and a public commitment. There seems to come a moment in the lives of people who choose to live together when they pause to reflect on their future life, and marriage seems the appropriate next step, the 'going up a gear'. But in other respects it is not unlike those occasions when a couple who have been married for many years want to reaffirm their marriage vows. It is in part a thanksgiving for their shared life to date but also a fresh commitment for the future and a desire to deepen the relationship further. The initiative for marriage in this parish comes usually from the woman. This is not to say that men are not enthusiastic or that they never make the running, but it is usually the woman who calls to make the initial arrangements. One woman said (and I have heard similar sentiments many times), 'I want him to know I really, really love him. And I want everyone else to know it as well.' It signifies a deepening of the bond.

This would be a reason for getting married anywhere, whether in church or not. What the church seems to be able to add to this is the language of the service, which articulates in a profound way what the couple think and feel. Marriage affects the way the couple tell the story of their own relationship. This is a commitment for a long period of time – 'till death us do part' – and through thick and thin. It is about sustaining a loving relationship over a life-time. It is a big deal. The church service says this aloud for the couple and is one reason why the church service is preferred to the more perfunctory alternatives. The act of getting married, the articulation of vows, the couple believes, deepens their relationship. What has gone before, one woman explained, was 'like a dress rehearsal'; now it is for real. We should not underestimate the power of the liturgy to articulate what couples want to say to one another in the presence of their families and friends. The Church literally gives them a voice at this crucial moment in their lives.

3. Security: 'for better, for worse'

If getting married is about deepening an already existing intimate relationship, it is also about seeking additional security by trying to guarantee the permanence and stability of it. One woman, who had worked in a circus for a number of years, put it to me this way: 'Getting married is like being on the high wire and deciding the time has come for a safety net.' It is mainly – though not entirely – the women who express themselves in this way. One man in his 30s said, half jokingly, that he wanted to 'get her to the altar' before all his hair fell out – his hairline was receding – and she started to 'look at other men'. The feeling is that getting married locks a couple more tightly into their relationship. They now commit themselves with solemn promises and before many witnesses to continue to share their lives with one another, come what may. The assumption, recognized but generally unspoken, is that the relationship is moving into phases where new strains will arise that will be more demanding – the arrival of children, a more exacting work life for one or both partners, less certain health or physical beauty. However, the vows, which is one of the few things that most couples seem to know about the service, speak of these realities. They do not paint marriage in idealistic and unreal terms but acknowledge ups and downs – for better as well as for worse, for richer as well as for poorer, in sickness as well as in health. Some of those 'downs' are just the sorts of situations that lead to the ending of relationships. But the vows make it clear that commitment in marriage is commitment to the other, whatever the quality of the relationship or the circumstances of the life together over a long period, over a life-time. As one man said,

'It means that if I get a brain tumour or something, she'll still be there for me.' That understanding of marriage is rightly regarded as a benefit without price. It is different from cohabiting, where the relationship is much more dependent on the continuing happiness of the partners. There seems to be an acceptance that married couples will show a greater preparedness to work through periods of difficulty than cohabiting couples, and there is some empirical evidence to suggest that couples are correct to think this.[18] Marriage does cause people to alter their behaviour. Men in particular become more responsible.[19]

When I ask people why they particularly want a church wedding, answers are often related to the notion of security. A young man said, 'I don't think weddings take in hotels.' The church wedding is perceived as a serious occasion and the ceremony is conducted with due and appropriate solemnity so that the marriage 'takes'. The marriage with its important vows is seen as supporting the relationship. (This is often denied. Love supports marriage and not vice versa, is the claim.)

For the women, the arrival of children is often a factor tipping the balance in favour of marriage. If a woman loses her financial independence in order to bring up a family, that creates some underlying anxiety about her vulnerability should her partner prove unreliable. The arrival of children begins to put a new strain on the relationship and men are often less able or less willing to cope. For the mother at home, marriage is a pair of handcuffs that binds a husband more tightly not just to her but to her and the children. From her point of view it is a form of informal social control, allowing her to be bolder in suggesting how he should behave towards his family.

It would be quite untrue to say that secular alternatives do not take marriage seriously. But there is something about the solemn rituals of the Church that help couples to appreciate that what they are doing is a serious matter. The wedding can be conducted in a relaxed way. There is a place for humour. But the language of the rite sounds the note of seriousness, which is what couples want. One young soldier compared his wedding with various formal military occasions he took part in, including the annual Remembrance Day parade. His partner, sitting beside him, accused him of being 'not very romantic' but he meant that these were serious occasions that required appropriate venues and rituals. His partner then agreed, adding, 'A church wedding is a proper wedding. I never quite believe a wedding in a hotel is a proper one. Hotels are for, well, a night out and enjoying yourself.'

When preparing couples for the wedding service I spend some time talking through the marriage vows. The church vows speak lyrically yet powerfully about the realities of life together. As we discuss them, it is not unusual for a couple to take each other's hand. The marriage vows speak not just about the ideal of marriage but also about the realities of the praxis of marriage. Marriage is a life-long commitment, yet it will have its ups and downs.

The desire for security is, however, undermined by an equal desire that marriage should not become oppressive for either partner and, that if it does, divorce should be easily available and no stigma should attach to it. Couples often have friends who are divorced or separated. They believe they should not be judgemental towards those who have left married partners. Yet if marriage is to offer a greater guarantee of permanence such attitudes towards those who break their marriage vows are hardly supportive. In traditional communities the security of marriage was reinforced by the stigmatization of the divorcee.

The seriousness of Christian marriage is also important to divorced people. Many of those married at St George's are divorced, and some, who have not lived in the parish, have made considerable sacrifices of time and commitment in order to be allowed on the electoral role. They often approach the clergy with considerable anxiety. They may not know whether or not their local vicar will agree to their marriage in church, nor whether he will be judgemental about their past marriage. I have heard some church members say they cannot understand why a person who has been divorced should want to get married in a church. The suggestion seems to be that a broken marriage is itself proof of a lack of commitment to the Church's understanding of marriage as a life-long partnership. The person who is divorced may have a real desire for a relationship that is enduring, and the Church's teaching about the life-long nature of a marriage is exactly what they believe and want.

In addition, the Christian faith offers something else that some divorced people need: forgiveness for past mistakes and the possibility of starting afresh, unencumbered by guilt. The priest does not necessarily have to hear a confession in any formal sense. A wedding in the setting of a church confers forgiveness for past wrongs and mistakes – that is what churches stand for – and enables a fresh start to be made. Neither the register office nor the hotel can do this. (It would be a mistake to assume that everyone will think this way. Those, for example, who have been very badly treated by their former spouse may experience only liberation and thankfulness.)

These are the reasons why people wear special clothes and want lots of flowers and spend considerable sums of money which, in this parish, they can often ill afford. It is to emphasize the importance of this occasion and to make it more memorable.

4. A sacred place

People want to get married in a church because it is a 'sacred place'. They want to get married in St George's because it is *their* 'sacred place'. For many people a particular 'sacred place' is important in their identity. A place is sacred because it is associated with serious and significant events in the life of a person or their family. A graveyard, or a particular grave, for example, is a sacred place: this is where parents or grandparents or brothers or sisters or children are buried. It is somewhere to visit and to be still and to reflect on lives lived and all that they meant. St George's Church is a sacred place for many people because this is where one or both of those being married was baptized. It is where their parents were married and where their grandparents' funerals were held. This is why, even though they may have moved away, they want to return to be married and, in time, may want to have their children baptized here. Being married in this place, which is sacred for them, is part of what I mean by cultural Christianity.

Sometimes clergy try to resist this, telling people to marry (and have children christened) at the church in the parish where they now live. But, as I have argued, this is to misunderstand the way in which many people associate with Christianity. If they were churchgoers they might well be married or have their children baptized locally – as members of that congregation. A local church, however, does not function for non-churchgoers in the way that their original church does. What is a sacred place for them is not any building where Christians gather to break bread, but a particular building associated with family events.

But what makes this a *sacred* and not just a familiar place? It is a sacred place because the rites here are Christian and they would count themselves as Christian even though they never attend church. I commented in Chapter 2 on the need each of us has to be able to place the story of our individual life within some wider understanding of the world and the meaning of human life. Individual narratives need to be set in some bigger narrative. Those who choose to be married in church, however inarticulate they may be, are acknowledging that they make sense of their lives by means of the Christian narrative. In the context of a marriage, those who come to St George's are wanting to hear again that marriage is 'a gift of God in creation'. It is something good – 'God-given' – that has enabled men and women to flourish, to live faithfully together and to raise children successfully. It has stood the test of time. This is expressed in many ways. For example, in recent marriages people have chosen hymns, readings and recorded music that all express in one way or another some of these themes. I asked one woman why she wanted to sing 'All things bright and beautiful' at her wedding. I thought she would say it was because she sang it at school. In fact she said, 'I think God meant getting married to be something bright and beautiful', which surprised me. Another woman asked for a reading and produced from a purse a cutting from a girl's magazine. She must have possessed it for years; it was very creased and difficult to read. It was a rather sentimental poem about marriages in church being blessed by God and so more secure. Her boyfriend, not without a slight hint of anger, said the piece of paper meant more to her than any present he had ever given her.

Instead of moaning and complaining, priests and congregations should rejoice that so many people understand themselves to be Christian and seek their sacred places for the various rites of passage.

Conclusion

In a comparatively short period marriage has gone from being a 'given' relationship to that of a more 'negotiated' one. At the same time older patterns of courtship have given way to newer patterns of living together, at least until the decision is made to have children. While most people value the freedom that these changes have brought, there are anxieties about the instability of many modern marriages.

The church wedding is valued because the Church takes marriage, which is understood as moving beyond cohabitation, seriously. It has something to say about the meaning of this relationship. Perhaps what the Church above all needs to articulate at this juncture, when the notion of the 'pure relationship' is powerful, is that this most intimate of relationships will inevitably have ups and downs: it will not be emotionally satisfying and enriching for both partners all the time. There will be times when the conflicting demands of being a partner, a parent and a person are not easy to reconcile and have to be worked out; there will be times when sustaining love will be difficult, when forgiveness has to be sought and granted. The Church knows these things, which is why its liturgy speaks about 'for better for worse, for richer for poorer, in sickness and in health'. The Church has the potential for further wisdom, but only if it can accept the changing patterns and work hard to understand how they can be made to work with and not against the idea of marriage as a life-long commitment. Articulating that wisdom is the challenge facing us.

5

Why funerals are overwhelmingly Christian

Parting is all we know of heaven,
And all we need of hell.
Emily Dickinson, 'My life closed twice before its close'

The changing scene

Why are most funerals presided over by clergy if we live in a secular age? The question is such an obvious one that it rarely gets asked. When it is asked, it is usually answered inadequately. For instance, it is sometimes said that when a death occurs people are in such a state of shock that they have no time to consider what the alternatives might be and are 'bounced' into a Christian funeral. It is true that funeral directors will move quickly to make arrangements, but they know that not discerning the wishes of the bereaved is, in the end, bad for business. It is also true that those most closely concerned may be in varying degrees of shock, but they, or those around them, are rarely so shocked that they cannot think at all about what they want to happen at the funeral of their loved one. It is also said that there are few alternatives to having a Christian minister involved. This is true; but it rather begs the question. In our consumer-oriented society, if there really were a sizeable demand for secular or humanist funeral services it is inconceivable that such a demand would not have been met by now. In urban areas the bigger firms of funeral directors would certainly be able to supply a secular 'master of ceremonies', and humanist forms of ceremony are easily obtainable. In any event, as people live longer they have more time to think about their own funerals, and they quite often do, telling relatives what they do and do not want. More people are beginning to plan their funerals, with suggestions for what might be read, who might speak, what music they want and where they want the overall emphasis to fall. Increasingly they want the occasion to be a 'celebration of their life', with grief swallowed up in thankfulness and cheerful recollection. But, while the number of humanist funerals is increasing, most people still seem content with adaptations of church funerals rather than some secular commemoration. The truth is that at present, the funeral services offered by the Christian churches are an acceptable ministry for the majority of the population. It might not always be so.

In this chapter I try to tease out why the vast majority of funerals in my parish continue to be according to religious rites of one sort or another. What does the religious funeral provide that secular funerals do not?

Principal trends to 1980

I begin, however, by noting some of the principal changes in the patterns of dying and grieving over the past half century and the way this has affected the funeral service.[1]

First, the creation of the National Health Service after the Second World War, combined with other improvements in the standard and quality of living, meant that people began to live longer lives and to die at a relatively advanced old age from degenerative diseases. In every century before this, people had died at home, often young or very young – they died as children, from illnesses that could not be cured or because medical help could not be afforded, in childbirth, as a result of poor diet, from industrial accident. In other words, life had been a perpetual struggle, death never seemed far away, and few lived into advanced old age. Death was often sudden and unexpected. It was certainly familiar. In life we were in the midst of death.

After the war, with better diets, better housing, free medical care and safer workplaces, life expectancy was dramatically improved. If a typical death before the war had been from some sudden, untreatable illness in childhood, after the war it was more likely to be as a result of cancer or heart disease in old age.

But as people lived longer and caring for them became more onerous, the tendency was for them to be admitted to more remote nursing homes and hospitals, so that dying now happened away from home, family and community. This had a number of consequences. Dying became more impersonal, on some anonymous Nightingale Ward, with curtains drawn around a bed. Death became something unfamiliar to families and communities, with fewer people ever seeing a dead body other than that of their husband or wife or parent, and not necessarily even then. While families visited the dying, the wider community often ceased to play a role since it had no knowledge of what was happening. Consequently, grieving was done alone or within the immediate family: bereavement became an increasingly lonely affair.

Table 4: Life expectancy (in years) at birth (Great Britain)

	1841	1901	1931	1961	1981	1991	2002
Men	41	45	58	67	70	73	76
Women	43	49	62	73	76	78	81

Data from the Office for National Statistics

In the second place, the links between death, the local community and the church all broke down. When people died at home, the neighbourhood knew and rallied round. They provided support for the family as a loved one was dying and support afterwards as they grieved. There were also traditional ways in which local communities expressed their sorrow and sympathy when death occurred – drawing curtains, sending wreaths, having a collection, standing at the front door to watch a hearse pass by, wearing black. Individual grieving could be swallowed up in communal mourning. Often, local clergy would become involved before the death, either because a family contacted them, or because neighbours asked them to call. Clergy might prepare the dying or say prayers with the family. But when people lay dying in hospital, the over-riding concerns were medical rather than spiritual. Doctors and nurses saw their principal role in terms of easing pain and making the patient physically comfortable. Preparing people spiritually for their death was not a duty that nurses relished taking on, even though the spiritual care of patients might be part of their job description. If they felt that spiritual help was needed, they would send for the hospital chaplain, if one were available, not the local minister. 'Spiritual' was understood to mean 'religious', and religion was thought to be the business of religious professionals. Because the contact with local churches and their clergy was now so attenuated, the traditional, religious understanding of what a 'good death' might mean was lost. A good death was a death free from pain. Death was medicalized and secularized.

The role of the local church was also affected by changes in the pattern of the disposal of the dead. In the post-war period, local authorities began to encourage cremation at the expense of burial by policies of differential fees. Burials were too costly: they took too much valuable land and they were labour intensive. Funeral directors also much preferred to take a body direct to a crematorium for the service and committal, rather than divert first to a local church, since that involved more than one journey and one unloading of the hearse. For a while in the 1950s and 1960s many thousands of services were held in crematoriums at which the officiating priest was not the local vicar but a clergyman who happened to be on a rota that week. Many of these rota services were poor and inadequate as a result. I remember doing 'cremation duty' a week at a time twice a year for several years as a curate in the late 1960s and early 1970s. It meant that the officiant knew almost nothing about the deceased, other than the name and age, and had no prior contact with the family. The situation has now improved so that local clergy take services of people from their parish and are able to visit the bereaved beforehand. Even so, the majority of services take place in the crematorium rather than the parish church. This makes it harder for the local church to become a focus for people's grieving.

The hospice movement and the turn to the self

The period 1950–1980 was marked, then, by the medicalization and secularization of death, the impersonality of dying, the loss of communal mourning and the loneliness of bereavement. But more recently there has been something of a reaction, and other trends can be discerned.

The hospice movement, for example, was a response to these trends and has had a considerable impact on the care of the dying, though the actual numbers of people dying in hospices has always been comparatively small.[2] After pioneering a great deal of palliative care for the terminally ill – such as pain management – more recently hospices have turned their attention to helping people die in their own homes surrounded by family and friends. The hospice movement has encouraged people to prepare again for death. But this preparation has not necessarily been traditionally religious.

One effect of the period from the founding of the NHS to the beginning of the present century has been, as we have seen, to distance the Church from those dying. Once those links had been broken they were not re-established. The hospice movement, while not hostile to traditional religion – many hospices had a religious foundation – was influenced by the prevailing culture and what we have termed the 'turn to the self' and the therapeutic sensibility. 'Spirituality' now came to be understood not as synonymous with religion but almost in contrast to it. 'Religion' was what happened in churches: it was about creeds and liturgies, set prayers, sacraments and clergy. But 'spirituality' was about inner experience: it was about how each individual faced up to and made sense of death in his or her own way. It was not about conforming to some established religious tradition. Spirituality became 'bespoke' rather than 'off the peg', '*à la carte*' rather than '*table d'hôte*'. It was also about dealing with the emotions – fear of dying, loss of dignity and the sense of self-worth, anxieties about loved ones, feelings of meaninglessness. The effect of all this can be seen in the requests that clergy now have for the inclusion of every kind of secular music and non-scriptural readings in services as well as tributes and forms of address that are very different from the traditional funeral sermon.

The bereaved

At the same time, there has been a growing recognition of the needs of the bereaved. While this is to be welcomed, there is a question as to whether the therapeutic culture does not sometimes disable rather than enable people. One feature of the therapeutic culture, as we have noted, is its low view of the emotional capacity of people to deal with life's mundane knocks, such as the death of a loved one. As people began to expect that everyone should live into old age, any death that fell short of three score years and ten was thought likely to 'traumatize' the relatives. Since people have a way of living up to expectations, this was probably a prophecy that fulfilled itself. It is now widely assumed that a death of anyone other than those in advanced age will 'devastate' the bereaved and that they will need help in coming to terms with their loss, working through their grief and 'letting go' their loved one. It is certainly the case that whenever a tragic death occurs – the death of a child, death from violence, death involving large numbers of people, and so on – counselling is now routinely offered.

It is instructive here to compare what happened after a major disaster involving the deaths of many children at Aberfan in 1966 with what happened after the death of children in later tragedies, such as that at Dunblane in 1996 and Soham in 2002.[3] Aberfan was the scene of a particularly devastating industrial accident, when a spoil heap from a local coal mine slid towards the village and engulfed the primary school. A total of 116 children and 28 adults died. How did people cope? Essentially, the village decided that it would cope through existing mechanisms of family and neighbourhood support. These were all the resources anyone would need, even for so terrible a disaster. Outside, 'expert' intervention was not sought. Two weeks after the accident the school reopened and the children went back to their books. The villagers believed that getting back to normal life was the way to take the minds of the children off the tragedy. They did not presume that anyone would be 'scarred for life'.

But by the time the Dunblane and Soham deaths occurred, it was widely assumed that people would not be able to cope without some intervention. Counselling is now routinely available whenever such disasters occur, and the authorities would probably feel open to criticism, and possibly to legal redress, if they failed to make the offer. The reaction of the people of Aberfan would be regarded now as eccentric or even callous.[4] Yet until the later decades of the twentieth century, that was how people coped. The prevailing attitude prior to that is caught in these remarks of the maid to her grieving mistress in a 1927 novel by Edith Olivier:[5]

'Try and get to bed, Miss,' she said. 'I know what you must be feeling, but you mustn't give way. Time will cure. Shall I make you a nice cup of tea?'

At any rate, by the beginning of the present century, the needs of bereaved people had been subject to a great deal of research and scrutiny, and it had been concluded that meeting those needs was more difficult as people began to live more private lives.

The funeral service

The Church has also sought to respond to change in its liturgies, and we can see this in the evolution of the funeral service over the past half century. It is instructive to compare the Book of Common Prayer's very brief burial service with the forms of service now in use in the contemporary Church. The language of the Prayer Book service is focused on the reality of death and the transition of the immortal soul from the miseries of this world to the joy and felicity of heaven. There is little or no consideration of the life the person has lived. When life in this world is mentioned in the prayers and readings, a rather gloomy view of it prevails; there is little to be thankful about. This is a sinful world and the best we can hope for is that we too shall soon be delivered from the burden of the flesh. In so far as the bereaved are considered, their comfort is assumed to lie in the knowledge that the dead, who rest now in God, will be raised up on the day of resurrection.

After the opening sentences, the service begins with two psalms that contrast God's abiding and eternal presence with the shortness of human life and its dreadful endpoint in death:

O spare me a little, that I may recover my strength: before I go hence, and be no more seen. (Psalm 39.15 BCP)

We bring our years to an end, as it were a tale that is told.
The days of our age are threescore years; and though men be strong, that they come to fourscore years: yet is their strength then but labour and sorrow; so soon passeth it away, and we are gone. (Psalm 90.9–10 BCP)

Consolation follows in the form of a long reading from Paul's first letter to the Corinthians, in which he explains how the faithful dead will be raised after an interval of 'sleep' at the coming of the risen Lord, to be clothed with their spiritual bodies. The funeral party then proceed to the grave for the words of committal. The Lord's Prayer is then said followed by two final prayers, in the second of which the mourners are reminded of Paul's words that they are not to be sorry 'as men without hope'.

When we turn to modern liturgies, we find differences of emphasis. *Common Worship*, for example, gives the reasons for the funeral as commending the deceased to God, but also 'to remember' the deceased and give thanks for his life. The Prayer

Book emphasis on the stark reality of death – as found in the two psalms – is more muted in *Common Worship*. The printed psalm is Psalm 23 (The Lord is my shepherd), which has a more gentle reference to 'the valley of the shadow of death'. The emphasis on remembrance of the life lived formed no part of the Book of Common Prayer service; but the modern funeral is often built around that theme. Bereaved relatives will often say they want the service to be a 'celebration of her life'. The concern for the life lived reflects a waning of interest in the life to come. The assumption of the newer forms seems to be that if there is less certainty about that, the less said the better. In some urban settings, a memorial service has begun to take the place of the funeral as the occasion when the wider circle of friends and the community pay their respects. The funeral then becomes a private and often quite brief affair. The memorial service, at which there is no body, is not then a rite of passage for the dead but can be given over completely towards the recollection of the life.

But the greatest contrast between traditional forms of funeral service and the contemporary is the way in which the contemporary forms have been influenced and shaped by the therapeutic culture – the emotions of the mourners are kept constantly in view. Modern liturgists would probably concur with Wesley Carr, who said that funerals are for the living.[6] So we find there is much greater provision for different kinds of death and what are presumed to be, therefore, different kinds of emotional responses on the part of those who are grieving. *Common Worship* has services for the funeral of a child as well as prayers 'After a short life', 'After a sudden death', 'After a violent death', 'After a suicide', 'After a long illness', 'In sorrow, guilt and regret'. In addition, the introduction to the service uses explicit psychological language to describe grieving as 'a process marked by different stages': special services and resources are provided 'in which some of these different stages can be recognized, spoken of in advance or recapitulated'.[7]

Other traditions have even more provision of this kind. The

Book of Common Order of the Church of Scotland, for example, has provision for the funeral of a still-born child, where the
introduction concerns itself directly with the emotions of those
grieving:[8]

> We gather here on what is for all of us a sad occasion. We
> were looking forward to a time of joy and happiness, and
> now there are tears and grief. We are left with a feeling of
> emptiness. All that has happened seems futile and pointless.
> Our minds are filled with questions to which there appear to
> be no answers: so many things we do not know; so many
> things we do not understand . . .

Four reasons for Christian funerals

There have, then, been considerable changes in just over half a
century in the way we come to die, the way we dispose of our
dead and the way we grieve. Even so, the majority of funerals
remain religious. What, then, are people looking for from the
Christian funeral? In other words, what would a Christian service provide that would be absent from a secular form? Let me
draw on my own experience to illustrate the points I would
make. Again, the point needs to be made that these observations
arise out of a particular parish in the north-west of England.

1. Keeping the door open

The first reason for people continuing to accept a Christian
funeral is that the religious funeral can be an open-ended occasion rather than a closed one. That is to say, the secular funeral
closes the door on any possibility of a life beyond this one. The
religious funeral keeps that door ajar. The secular funeral says,
'This world is all there is.' The religious funeral says, 'There are
more things in heaven and earth . . .'. How many more will vary
from rite to rite, minister to minister, and in accordance with the
wishes of the deceased. The funeral of a practising member of a
congregation can see the door to eternal life flung wide open

with a confident assertion in hymn and reading and prayer of the resurrection life in the nearer presence of God. A religious funeral can also be more cautious; but doors are never wholly closed.

In older rites, the coffin containing the dead body was the focus, and the language of the rite spoke unequivocally and principally about transition from this world to the next. It was above all else a rite of passage for the deceased. This was especially true when the method of disposal was burial rather than cremation and the form of service was from the Book of Common Prayer. The Order for the Burial of the Dead is very short, allowing for the whole of the service to take place at the graveside, where the coffin is central. Both the centrality of the coffin and the words of the liturgy leave mourners in no doubt that what they are doing is taking part in a ritual marking the transition of the one who has died from this world to the next. While the body of the deceased is lifeless and must be returned to the ground, their immortal soul passes into the nearer presence of God. In that sense the traditional funeral looked forwards rather than back, to the life of the world to come rather than the life lived on earth.

In modern services, however, there is a move away from the main or only focus being on the dead body and the passage of the soul to its heavenly resting place. Contemporary rituals tend to have two rather different emphases. First, there is a concentration not so much on the departed as dead, nor on the transition to another life, as on the life that the departed has lived. In that sense the modern funeral looks back rather than forwards. Sometimes this is signalled on a service sheet that describes what is happening not as a funeral but as a 'celebration' of the deceased's life. This shift of emphasis is aided in some crematoriums by the coffin being placed off-centre, with the centre of focus becoming those who pay tribute to the life lived. It is also reflected in a growing trend in some urban areas, especially London, to hold a small, private cremation for the immediate family, followed at a later date by a memorial service for everyone else. On these occasions the coffin is not present at all and the whole emphasis is on thanksgiving for the life. The second focus of the modern funeral service is the bereaved. As we have seen, most contemporary rites acknowledge the needs of the bereaved at several points and turn the service in effect into a rite of passage for the bereaved rather than for the dead person.

Even so, the Church's funeral rites continue to speak unambiguously about death as the gateway to another life. In my experience, this is exactly the focus that the majority of people continue to want and a major factor in their being content to have a Christian funeral. The evidence for this is not easy to find because it is not something that the religious sociologist is particularly schooled to observe: it runs against the secularization thesis. But clergy who visit at the time of a death know that mourners often indicate that they do believe their loved ones live on in some other realm, or at least they have not closed their mind to the possibility. These are remarks that have been made to me in the very recent past, all from non-churchgoers: 'She's gone to a better place'; 'He's with our mam now' (a daughter speaking about the death of her father); 'We want to give him a good send off' (the deceased's workmates speaking about their wish to be involved in the service – the suggestion is that he is continuing a journey, not that he has ceased to exist).

We could also look at some of the sentiments that people write on cards with floral tributes or in the obituary notices of newspapers. These are a few recent comments from wreathes at funerals in my parish, again of non-churchgoers:

'Till we meet again' (from a wife to her husband of 60 years); 'Look after her, Jesus' (from the sister of a young woman in her 20s); 'Safe in God's arms. Night, night. God bless. Nana.'

The obituaries in the local newspaper also give some clues about beliefs that are normally kept well-hidden. Some of these are explicitly Christian, others are less so, though one can discern roots in more orthodox belief. Many speak of God 'calling' or 'taking' the deceased. If this is after a painful illness or a difficult life, there is the idea that God will now ease pain and offer protection. In general the belief is that death is the gateway to a life free from pain in God's nearer presence, with a confidence that the dead have passed to this new life. Sometimes this is called heaven. In this new life the recently departed will at once recognize those loved ones who have preceded them and will wait until those who are left behind join them. If this seems to be the most widely held belief, there are variations. There is the suggestion that the dead do not go to some supernatural realm but are our silent and unseen companions on life's journey. There is also the idea that the dead are 'sleeping' until that day in some indeterminate future when they will awaken to meet those loved ones whom they preceded (which is much closer to orthodox Christianity):[9]

> Each time I see your picture
> You seem to smile and say
> Don't cry, I'm only sleeping
> We'll meet again some day.

Other beliefs also surface from time to time. Sometimes I meet people who say they have been influenced by Indian religions and believe in reincarnation. Sometimes a bereaved family will want to read some piece of new age mysticism about the spirit of the deceased emptying out in the natural world – in the stars or the sunlight or the flowers in the woodland. None of this suggests a wholly secularized people, though much of the talk about woods and flowers and sunlight is often just a gentler way of speaking about the non-existence of dissolution. Even so, much of what people want to say does not suggest a complete turn from the possibility of another world of existence to this.

What is also very interesting to note is that people often speak in this fashion in the context of arranging the funeral but would not spend very much time, if any at all, expressing these sentiments in any other context. They might even be quite embarrassed if they were raised in another situation. They lie somewhere in the back of the mind, a pool of notions that can be drawn upon at the appropriate time.

Those who espouse such beliefs want a religious funeral because even where they know that what they believe is not the teaching of the Church, they instinctively feel that they will have a more sympathetic hearing in a religious setting than in a secular one. Local knowledge will tell people that at St George's attempts will be made to acknowledge the variety of views that may exist within particular families. All of this points to the importance of the pre-funeral visit and attentive listening to what the bereaved are trying to say.

2. Not letting go the dead

The secular world dismisses any idea of a life beyond this one. As a result, the appropriate response to death is to grieve for the one who has been lost in death, and to learn how to 'let go' of that person. Failure to do this is 'pathological'. This has been the focus of grief counselling for the past 20 years. In the 1980s I can remember bereavement counsellors addressing ordinands in training on the need for 'grief work' to be undertaken. This was a relatively aggressive approach to people 'stuck in denial' to get them to 'move on' and give up trying to cling to the memory of their dead loved ones. They could not hope for 'resolution' (it is now called 'closure') as long as they continued to pine for the deceased. A kind of Buddhist detachment was to be aimed at. The ordinands were told to look for the signs of morbidity: 'excessive' crying, hanging on to clothes, turning bedrooms into shrines, and so on. Above all, the passage of time should lead to the drastic diminution of such morbid clinging to the dead. 'Letting go' was the objective of the tasks of grief work.

Over the years, I have met a large number of bereaved people who have wanted to have some continuing relationships with their dead loved one but have been inhibited from saying so or from revealing their need to others. This is a consequence of years of secular counselling. One woman I visited, for example, kept her husband's ashes in a vase on the mantelpiece. She eventually told me, shyly and not without difficulty, that she 'talked' to her husband – that is, the vase containing the ashes – every day. It eased her loneliness. Yet when she had mentioned this to one of her daughters, she had told her it was morbid. So she had never mentioned it again. This is where our more secular culture leaves so many people.

But the Christian religion does not speak about 'letting go' the deceased. Rather it allows a new relationship to be made with them. In the High Anglican tradition, as in Roman Catholicism, there can be a straightforward praying for the dead. The dead are understood to be alive in another realm, and they are able to be 'reached' by the prayer of the faithful. Prayer allows those who pray to go on thinking of the well-being of their loved ones and to go on offering them their loving concern. If prayer puts the people praying into the direct presence of God, they are comforted in knowing that their loved ones are also in that same presence. It is simply that the veil of sense hangs dark between. For Roman Catholics, masses can be said for the dead as well as prayer offered.

Those who are not regular churchgoers understand very well that the Christian funeral will express the idea of a continuing relationship with the dead. Part of the task of the minister is to show how this can be done through prayers that speak of the reality and finality of death, but also enable a new caring relationship in prayer to begin. Some churches are able to offer prayer at particular times – an annual commemoration, perhaps at Easter or All Souls-tide – while others have memorial books and a year's mind or yearly remembrance at the main Sunday service. In a more secular culture, showing people that they do not have to 'let go' their dead in some absolute sense may be one of the most important services the Church can render.

3. Non-utilitarian assessment of human life

The religious funeral offers a religious evaluation of a person that may be very different from the utilitarian assessment of human lives of a secular culture.

We have noted a tendency in modern funerals for the emphasis to be on the life lived rather than the soul's transition to the next world. This is all very well if the life lived has been a reasonably long one and everyone can feel that it has been a worthwhile one. But this is never going to be universally true. As I look back over my own ministry I can recall some very difficult funerals where celebrating a life lived was either challenging or simply impossible. What is there to say about a still-birth? What can we say about an anencephalic baby born with little or no brain who lived for a few hours? We can say that the nine months of waiting for the child had brought much happiness, but that would only make the death seem even more cruel and tragic. What can we say about a young man whose life had been marked by dropping out of school, never holding down a job, failing with all his attempted relationships, sinking into depression and alcoholism, botching an attempt at suicide and finally wandering drunk into the path of an on-coming lorry? A memorial service and a funeral service that seeks to celebrate the life of the deceased is contingent on people being able to feel that the positive aspects outweighed, or at least made up for, the negative. But some people's lives can be nasty, brutish or short – or all three. In fact, many lives can have within them periods that no one particularly wants to call to mind or aspects of character that are deeply flawed. There are skeletons in many cupboards, shameful events in many lives.

There are also some influential secular voices that are actively calling now for the Christian or religious assessment of human life to be abandoned. Peter Singer, the philosopher, is quite clear that once the religious assessment of human beings is given up it enables us to see in a more clear-sighted way that we do not in fact treat all human lives as of equal worth. He proposes a new commandment – 'recognize that the worth of human life varies' – in place of the old – 'treat all human life as of equal worth'.[10] This makes it easier for us to take decisions to end the lives of anencephalic or cortically dead infants and patients in a persistent vegetative state. The danger with such a utilitarian approach is that it builds pressure on other lives whose quality is judged less than desirable – the frail elderly, the badly disabled, the chronic sick. A non-religious funeral has to find positive things to say about a life lived: a Christian funeral says of every person, however the quality of their life has been assessed by the human community, that this too was 'a child of God'.

The Christian funeral service does not seek to pretend that every life is or can be made to seem wonderful. Rather, the Christian account speaks of people being made in the image and likeness of God but also marred by sin. None is perfect, though all human lives are capable of redemption. The world itself awaits its redemption. Part of what this suggests is that we should resist placing the entire emphasis of the address on the life of the deceased; and where a tribute is given by a family friend there should also always be a sermon.

4. Tying up loose ends

One danger with the secular funeral is that it tends to make the bereaved more central, but it may be unable to deal effectively with the raw feelings and loose ends that so frequently accompany a death. The religious funeral service is able to deal with difficult emotions and to help to tie up loose ends.

As people live longer the possibility of putting one's affairs in order and saying farewells is becoming more common. (One woman in her 90s whom I saw each month with house communion did say, however, that she had grown weary with saying goodbyes.) Even so, there are still many deaths that are unexpected and unprepared for. A satisfactory funeral rite needs to be able to take this into account.

For example, there are many who die with things unsaid. There are also those who die having said harsh and unpleasant things to those around them, or who die unreconciled. This means that people come to the funeral with raw emotions, feelings of guilt. When someone takes their own life, powerful emotions are stirred in those close to the suicide. People feel bad and guilty: Why didn't we notice? Or, noticing: Why didn't we do something or something more? Or they may feel angry: How could he do this to us who loved him? They may also feel now one emotion, now another. There is no way that these feelings can be dealt with by the deceased. If guilt is to be forgiven and anger understood and forgiven, only the language of liturgy and prayer will do. In the absence of the deceased, only God can forgive. In the funeral service there is a form of confession and absolution. There are also prayers that the 'memories of hurt and failure' may be forgiven, as well as time for private prayer.

The experienced pastor will know how important a time of silent reflection can be. People need time to gather scattered thoughts and make some sense of conflicting emotions. But one feature of the funeral service at a crematorium is the comparative brevity of the service. There are still crematoriums where the time allowed is as little as 20 minutes.

Appreciating what loose ends may be around in any given funeral is an important part of pastoral ministry and one that is valued. In this parish I think of the following occasions and their complex loose ends and mixed emotions:

- The suicide of a teenager following accusations of bullying at school and alleged failure to act on the part of teachers.
- The death of a well-liked, physically disabled woman whose husband was known to have a mistress and whose adult children were all very disapproving of their father.
- A young man killed in a road accident in which he had caused severe and permanent injuries to another.

It is hard to believe that a secular funeral in some distant crematorium could be as helpful, not just to the immediate family, but also to a wider section of the community, as a religious service conducted in the local church by the local priest armed with local knowledge.

Conclusion

We live in a culture that is more secular and that lays great stress on emotion and feelings. But secularism inevitably views death as the last word on human life, and while this may reflect the views of many in contemporary Britain, it does not reflect the views of all. The religious funeral service does not close off other possible meanings. In general, people are living longer and dying in old age. As they live longer they have time to prepare for their deaths. In the past, preparing for death would have been done within a framework provided by the Christian faith and with the help of Christian ministers. The Christian religion provided the meaning of life and death, and Christian ministers supplied scriptural texts, prayers and rituals. Today, when people die in hospital, doctors and nurses are ill-prepared and generally reluctant to help people with what is a spiritual task. When people die at home, they are increasingly wanting to make sense of death in their own way and with the help of family and friends rather than ministers and priests.

Sensitive and experienced pastors know well that, whenever a death occurs, a range of often conflicting emotions are in play. Some of these emotions will be known to the pastor and perhaps other mourners, some will not. But the funeral liturgy is able to help people deal with them – whether they are of sorrow, anger, frustration, fear, guilt – and find some consolation. It speaks of the reality of death and helps those who grieve not to be held in denial; but it also allows them to begin to see how a new relationship with the dead is possible in prayer. But the minister will also have to recognize that in today's culture, there will have to be more emphasis on the life of the deceased and on the emotions of the bereaved. We cannot pretend that belief in life after death is a deeply held belief; nor that there has not been a 'turn to the self'.

Part Three
The implications for the Church

~6~

Conclusions

'Tis but at best a narrow bound
That Heaven allows to men,
And pains and sins run through the round
Of three score years and ten.
Isaac Watts, 'Hosanna to Christ'

A time of no religion?

This final chapter summarizes what I have been saying by setting out a number of principles that I believe the contemporary
Church should have in mind as a guide for its life and mission
in the twenty-first century. I will lay these alongside what I
believe are undesirable tendencies that the Church is beginning
to show, which are the result of some inadequate readings of the
prevailing culture and the nature of the Church's mission and
ministry.

Two arguments have been running through this book. The
first is that the strong version of secularization theory is not
wholly persuasive. It does not capture accurately the culture of
contemporary British society. While it is true that many meas-
urable indices point to a falling away of churchgoing and a
decline in the Church's general influence in the public sphere,
nevertheless a majority of the British people stubbornly refuses
to be categorized as secular. On the contrary, the majority insists
on identifying with one or other of the major faiths, principally
Christianity. This is the finding of any number of opinion polls
and, more particularly, the national census. (The idea that
Britain is becoming inexorably more secular also takes insuffi-
cient account of the possible future impact of minority faiths,

especially Islam, among whose followers birth rates are higher than those of the population as a whole, and who seem able to induct their children successfully into the faith.) What the strong version of secularization theory does not explain, there-fore, is why people who are supposed to be so secularized – because they do not attend places of worship – continue to define themselves as religious. The conclusion we ought rather to draw from this, at least for the present, is that for many British people, failure to participate in the institutional life of the Church is not necessarily a sign that Christian faith has been repudiated. This is because participation in church life is not seen as crucial for the *practice* of Christianity, and it is the prac-tice of Christianity that British people think important. This is what makes a person a Christian, not churchgoing. (This is probably the legacy of a certain type of liberal Protestantism that emphasized altruism and good works.) If pressed they would say that this is the way of living that Jesus taught and exemplified. It has a moral and a spiritual dimension. I have called this 'cultural Christianity' to distinguish it from both institutional or churchgoing Christianity and from what is sometimes called 'implicit' religion – the idea that people are naturally spiritual and that this is the default position of human beings – for which I would not want to argue. We may sum-marize this by saying that while the British may lead more sec-ular lives, they retain sacred hearts.

The second argument has been that when the ministry of the Church is sought, that must have considerable significance in a more secular culture and a society where there are no social pressures to identify with the institutional church. This asking for ministry is more than just 'residual Christianity'. It is some-thing that the Church should take seriously or it will fail in its pastoral vocation.

If there is any force in these arguments then there are import-ant implications for the role of the Christian Church in the twenty-first century. In this chapter I shall try to bring this into sharper focus by describing what I think are certain tendencies

of the modern Church and setting out the alternative principles
that I believe should guide it instead. Behind all of this, however,
is an understanding of God and his relationship to the world
that now needs to be made more explicit, since it is that understanding that gives point and direction to everything else.

God, the world and the Church

A local church may relate to its community in one of two principal ways. On the one hand, it may take the view that a very
important part of its mission is to be concerned with the welfare
(in the broadest sense) of all those who live in its locality.
Churches that take this position tend to blur the line of demarcation between the church and the world. This is the 'parish
church' understanding of the role of the Church. On the other
hand, a church may see its task primarily in terms of bringing
people to Christian faith and making them part of the worship-
ping community. The line of demarcation between church and
world is now much sharper. This is the 'gathered church' model.
The two types are not necessarily wholly incompatible: it may
be a question of emphasis. The 'parish church' model has an
understanding of 'mission' that includes evangelism, though it
encompasses far more than that. The 'gathered church' model,
while not excluding social service, sees evangelism as the principal reason for the Church's existence. These differences supply
the overall rationale of a particular church and give dynamic
and coherence to its various activities. The danger for the
'parish church' is that its members lose sight of the distinctive-
ness of Christianity and become unduly influenced by the values
of the wider community or dominant social group. The danger
for the 'gathered church' is that it equates repentance and faith
with churchgoing and becomes pharisaical and judgemental in
a way that Jesus in the Gospels criticised.

But as well as the attitude of the Church towards its local
community, there is also the attitude of the community towards
its local church. Some churches are almost invisible as far as the

locality is concerned; others may evoke feelings of respect or affection (or, of course, anger and annoyance) even though few people are regular attenders. These different attitudes are often revealed when attempts are made to close a local church. A planned closure may provoke little or no reaction or it may produce a storm of local protest. Behind these reactions lie years of a certain kind and level of engagement between the Church (clergy and laity) and its local community. These reactions also point to an important truth of human societies: we can feel that we have some stake in an institution such as a church even if we are not regular members of it.

It should be said that none of this is a matter of the particular form of governance of a church. Neither the denomination of a church, nor for that matter its style of worship, is necessarily a guide to the way it relates to its local community. Although historical Anglicanism has been of the 'parish church' type, there are an increasing number of Anglican churches that no longer see their role in these terms. Equally, while the Free Churches have generally been of the 'gathered church' type, some, especially Methodist churches and United Reformed churches, exercise a 'parish church' role in their localities. In one parish where I became vicar, a previous Methodist minister in the area had been known as 'the vicar' because he played a role in the local community that was consistent with a 'parish church' understanding. Each local church, then, of whatever denomination, lays down over time its own distinctive relationship with its locality.

Behind these two ways of being church are two different ways of understanding God and his relationship to the world. The 'parish church' model presupposes a God whose primary concern is the day to day welfare of all people in the present age. The emphasis is on Jesus as one who fed the hungry, healed the sick and raised up the poor, and in so doing revealed the nature of God as forgiving and loving and exemplified what the kingdom of God would be like when it came. The 'gathered church' model places the emphasis on the need for human beings to repent and turn to God. Jesus is principally understood as the prophet who came preaching repentance for sin and faith in him as the saviour. God is compassionate; but he is also a judge. Different ways of thinking about God and different theological emphases produce different ways of thinking about the role of the Church.

These different ways of being church and relating to the local community are not fixed for all time. A way of relating may wither through neglect or be changed as a result of deliberate policy. A 'parish church' type of local church, for instance, can cease to concern itself with local people and local issues, or can resolve to become more of a 'gathered church'. Major shifts in the status and position of Christianity in a culture will inevitably lead to a fresh consideration of the Church's role. It is often, however, the arrival of a new minister that is the catalyst for change one way or another.[1]

Tendencies and principles

In this book I have argued for a particular way of envisaging both God and his relationship to the world, and also the church and its relationship to its locality. However, the contemporary Church is marked by four tendencies, which, I believe, are beginning to take it in another direction. These tendencies need to be counteracted by alternative commitments – I call them principles – if the Church is to continue to serve the people of this country in the way that has been distinctive of the Church of England in the past and that, I believe, witnesses to something important about God himself.

First tendency of the contemporary Church:
Make a clear line of demarcation between 'the Church' and 'the world' and see the overriding task of the Church as evangelism.

First counteracting principle for the contemporary Church:
Recognize that not all Christians are members of the Church

and see the Church, including its occasional offices, as a spiritual resource for members and non-members alike.[2]

First of all we need to face a serious and difficult matter, namely the very existence of the Church. The trouble with the church is that it is a constant cause of embarrassment. As I write this, the Roman Catholic Church is desperately trying to deal with the scandal of child abuse by priests and religious in the USA and Ireland; the Anglican Communion is seeking to avoid giving way to homophobia; and all the churches are still wrestling with attitudes and patterns of behaviour inherited from a patriarchal past. How necessary, then, is the institutional church to Christianity? The question invites both a theological and a sociological response. Theologically the question can be reformulated as: Do you have to belong to the Church in order to be saved? Sociologically it is asking: Would Christianity continue to have influence in the culture even if the Church were to disappear? I believe Christians have to consider both questions.

St Augustine said that we would not have God as Father unless we had the Church as mother. Theologically, there have always been those Christians who have said that the Church is necessary for salvation. Some have said it is necessary in the sense that the Church is the irreplaceable conduit through which the Christian message is transmitted from generation to generation. There is undoubtedly truth in this. It is hard to see how Christianity could be sustained if there were not at least a nucleus of people who took some responsibility for transmitting the gospel to the next generation and also made some attempt to engage theologically with the issues that concern contemporary men and women. This is not an argument for any particular type of church or church organization, only that Christianity needs to take some institutional form. As with all institutions it will need to adapt to changing circumstances and from time to time it will need to be reformed. The guiding principle, or at least the minimum requirement, must be that, as far as humanly possible, the institutional form should not detract from the fundamental messages of the Christian faith. This is why bad behaviour on the part of the clergy – the public representatives of the Church – is such a scandal.

But others have argued for more than this: that 'outside the Church there is no salvation' – you cannot be saved other than by becoming a member of the church. Catholics who have thought along these lines have pointed to the need for sacramental grace, Protestants placed the emphasis on sitting under God's word as the people of God on the way to the Kingdom. Either way, a line of demarcation is drawn between those who are in the church (and therefore saved) and those who are in 'the world' (and therefore lost). The Church is then conceived as an ark, a place of safety. The ark may be tossed about on stormy seas, but it is able to hold the faithful few until God's intervention stills the storm and restores order. The biblical antecedent is the story of the flood and Noah's ark. The over-riding task of the church is to make continuous and strenuous efforts to save people from spiritual drowning.

This way of thinking has its attractions and in an uncertain and confused age it seems to offer clarity. There is 'the world' and there is 'the church', and you either belong to the one or the other. But it has its drawbacks. There is a theological argument about whether Jesus saw things this way. In his ministry he seems more concerned with belonging to the Kingdom than belonging to the Church, and he finds evidence of the Kingdom showing itself in all sorts of unexpected places and among all sorts of unlikely people. As a result, some have even contrasted the Kingdom and the Church. At the beginning of the last century, one theologian provocatively suggested that whereas Jesus promised the Kingdom, what we got was the Church. But leaving that aside, the trouble with any insistence that salvation is dependent on membership of the Church is that, as we have seen, the institutional church often looks more like a problem than a solution. This should at least make us cautious in our claims about the Church. Or rather, we should see some of the theological language about the Church not as a description of what the Church is actually like, but as an ideal to which it should aspire. We say that the Church is the body of Christ, not because for much of the time it remotely looks like it, but because this is the high ideal to which it is called. As a human institution it shares all the faults and failings of all human institutions. And because it also sees itself as a divine institution it can also be guilty of great arrogance, refusing to acknowledge and even excusing its faults and failings.

This leads to a second objection to this way of thinking. It assumes too easily that 'church' and 'world' can be separated out. As we noted in the discussion of baptism, there are some Christians who want to see a sharp divide between church and world, believer and non-believer. This is why they often accept very readily the findings of secularization theorists; they fit their own paradigm of the nation as utterly secular – by which they mean 'godless'. They believe the work of the Church is to draw people away from the pernicious influence of a godless culture into the safety of the Christian subculture. Mission, in the sense of evangelism, is the over-riding task, and ministry is simply another opportunity for converting people to churchgoing Christianity. I have argued throughout that this is a misreading of the culture. It also fails to recognize that the only way such absolute demarcations could be drawn would be by Christians retreating into self-contained enclaves, rather as the Amish and some Mennonites have done in the USA.

A 'softer' and very fashionable version of this is the suggestion that Christians are 'resident aliens' – in the world but not of it – and, being aliens, never really at home here. I doubt whether this is psychologically sustainable. If we are to flourish as individuals and if we are to enable our communities to flourish, we have to put down roots, which must be emotional as well as material. I doubt whether we could feel rooted if we also felt 'alien'. We need to hear the words of the prophet Jeremiah to the exiles in Babylon. They had cried the cry of the resident alien:

> By the waters of Babylon, we sat down and wept: when we
> remembered Zion . . . 'How can we sing the Lord's song in a
> strange land?' (Psalm 137.1, 4 ASB)

But the prophet will not let them live as resident aliens. They
are to put down roots, to live as residents, and seek the common
good of the place to which they have come:

> Thus says the Lord of hosts, the God of Israel, to all the exiles
> whom I have sent into exile from Jerusalem to Babylon: Build
> houses and live in them; plant gardens and eat their produce.
> Take wives and have sons and daughters; take wives for your
> sons, and give your daughters in marriage, that they may bear
> sons and daughters; multiply there, and do not decrease. But
> seek the welfare of the city where I have sent you into exile,
> and pray to the Lord on its behalf, for in its welfare you will
> find your welfare. (Jeremiah 29.4–7)

In its welfare you will find your welfare. This too is the
Gospel.

In any case, it is only too easy for Christians to think they
stand over against the prevailing culture while in fact they are
being influenced by it. Or rather, it is easy to strain at a gnat
and swallow a bird. So, for example, within the Church, Christians may resist giving homosexuals the equality they increasingly have in the wider society – on the grounds that they are
not going to be influenced by the values of an alien culture –
while at the same time allowing the culture of emotionalism to
influence quite uncritically worship styles and pastoral practice. The Church does not exist in an enclave and, therefore,
while it must witness to 'the world' it is also part of the world.
If the Church does not understand this it will fail to be alert to
the ways in which the culture may influence it, and it will fail
to see the opportunities that it must grasp in order to influence
the culture and to support those Christians who are not members of congregations.

So how necessary is the Church? From a sociological perspective we would have to say that some form of institution is necessary if Christianity is to be perpetuated and to continue to influence men and women. The Church seeks to influence men and women with the gospel of Jesus Christ through the way it is organized, through what it teaches, through its liturgy and through the life and witness of its members. If the institutional church were to disappear, the accumulated Christian capital of society would run down. There is already evidence of this happening as people cease to be churchgoing and as religious education in schools gets thinner and more fragmented. This also means that if the Christianity of those who are not church members is to be maintained, they too need the institutional church, even though they are reluctant to join it. The role of the Church, therefore, is not only to draw people into membership but also to sustain those who identify with Christianity but, for whatever reason, do not wish to become participating members of the Church on a regular basis.

In this respect, the role of the Church is not unlike the preaching and teaching ministry of Jesus himself. By being close to God he was able to recognize and point to the places where the Father was making himself known. Some of these occasions were in a religious context and some not. The Church needs to see itself not as the embodiment of the Kingdom but as serving the Kingdom that continues to break through in unexpected places. This is why the Church must take seriously those occasions when people do come to church. The hastily written funeral or wedding address or the poorly performed baptism are missed opportunities with serious consequences. If the clergy judge their 'success' at the occasional offices in terms of whether or not people are subsequently drawn into regular membership, they will often be left feeling that they have failed. But if they see each occasional office as an important moment in nourishing and educating the faith of those who are Christians though not regular churchgoers, then their approach would be transformed. They would grasp this opportunity for genuine ministry – and a very testing occasion for the minister at that. In a very short period of time in a very particular context he must say something that will be helpful to these people in their spiritual lives and also perform the ceremony in a way that does justice to the meanings embedded in the liturgy.

The first principle, then, is to recognize that not all Christians are members of the Church and to see the Church, including its occasional offices, as a spiritual resource for members and non-members alike.

Second tendency of the contemporary Church:
Assume that God wants everyone to become a member of the Church.

Second principle for the contemporary Church:
See Church membership as a particular vocation of some Christians for the sake of others.

Those who assimilate ministry to mission do so because they believe God wants everyone to become a member of the Church. Of course, I do not want to deny that anyone may become a member of the Church. Nor do I want to deny that the core convictions of Christianity are true and that the world needs to know these truths. Part of the vocation of the Church, therefore, must be to preach and teach the truths of the Christian faith and to bear witness to them in the way that its members live out their lives. But is this the same as saying everyone must become a member of the Church? The real danger with the position of those who say that evangelism is the primary function of the Church is that they are suggesting that becoming a Church member is the only way someone can 'repent and believe'. In his ministry Jesus seemed to find all sorts of people who were 'not far from the Kingdom of God' – yet this had little to do with their standing within Judaism. Indeed, some of them might not have been Jewish at all.

If we equate responding to the challenge of Jesus – the gospel – with 'becoming a member of the Church', a number of things follow. First, this could only be true if the Church were the perfect embodiment of the gospel. But we know that is not the case. The Church may be a divine institution in the sense that it is called into being by God; but that is very different from saying that it is a perfect society in which we are bound to flourish. We have seen the struggle the Church has had in our own day to retain credibility in the face of scandals. But even without these major instances of abuse and injustice, there is more than enough mundane pettiness to make the claim that God requires everyone to join the Church seem outlandish. We are forced to concede that not everyone will flourish as a result of Church membership. It must be possible for people to respond to the gospel but to say 'no thank you' to the Church.

Second, if we believe the only authentic response to the challenge of Jesus is to join the Church, we are destined to spend our Christian lives colluding in failure. Many people, perhaps most people, are not and will not be members of the Church. Historically, most people probably never were regular members of the Church. That did not prevent the Church exercising influence. So we need to shift the perspective and think of Church membership not as the vocation of all but as the vocation of some – on behalf of all. The task of those who are called to be churchgoing Christians is to help those who are not churchgoing but who still think of themselves as Christians, and those who may not think of themselves in this way at all, to 'repent and believe' in their own way.

What does all this mean in practice?

It means that the Church must seek to influence not only through what it teaches and preaches and what it proclaims in its liturgies and services, but also through the way its members live out the truth of the gospel in their day-to-day living. A Christian bank manager is not necessarily a better bank manager than the next bank manager, but he or she should seek to be the best bank manager he or she is capable of being –

conscientious, hard-working, having high standards and expectations, yet encouraging and supportive, and so on. In this way, Christians illustrate in their own living what the Church teaches, setting before their colleagues and neighbours living parables of what it means to live according to the gospel. This is to recover the Reformation understanding of 'vocation', 'calling'. Christians are called by God to be Christians in specific circumstances. As Luther pointed out, we all have several 'callings' – to be a husband or wife, a parent, a friend, a butcher, a baker, a candlestick maker.

This second tendency – assume that God wants everyone to become a member of the Church – has an important bearing on the question of the relationship between Christianity and other faiths. The tendency with the 'gathered church' model, and the theology that underpins it, is that it leads towards a devaluing of the spiritual contribution that other faiths might make. They are part of 'the world' from which women and men must be delivered if they are to be saved. This makes serious engagement with other faiths much more difficult, since serious dialogue means being willing to be changed in potentially significant ways as a result of what the other says. But if we view other faiths as so much worldly dross we will not want to listen, let alone learn. But if we are to have cohesive communities in pluralist Britain, the faith communities in urban centres will need to engage more and more in dialogue. That is easier to do if the tendency to assume that God can only countenance Christians is resisted.

The second principle is to see Church membership as a particular vocation of some Christians for the sake of others.

Third tendency of the contemporary Church:
Regard buildings as of secondary importance or even no importance at all in sustaining the spiritual life.

Third principle for the contemporary Church:
Recognize the vital role played by sacred buildings in sustaining the spiritual life of members and non-members.

There are powerful voices in the modern Church that would argue that buildings are not important. 'People before buildings' has become a cliché of contemporary Christianity. What is important, it is argued, is the conversion of souls and the worship of God, and this does not need a particular building or a building at all. Indeed, the buildings can become a snare and a delusion, draining people of time, energy and finance, turning Christians into museum keepers and distracting from the real business of evangelism.

There is obvious truth in some of this. Jesus in St John's Gospel says that true worship is not dependent on buildings but is a matter of spirit and truth (John 4.24). Yet the Lord is repeatedly found in both synagogue and temple, as were the first Christians. It also seems to be the case that once Christians were no longer welcome in synagogues they soon began to turn their meeting places into something more than a convenient place to gather. They created sacred spaces.

Of course, the contemporary Churches are not so replete with either members or money that they can be sentimental about their buildings. Hard choices do have to be made about adaptation and closure. But decisions are not necessarily right simply because they are painful. They are more likely to be wrong if taken in the belief that buildings are not important for sustaining souls.

There is a tendency in the modern Church to underestimate the role that the building can play in sustaining faith. For many contemporary Christians, what is important to them is the coming together of the Christian congregation for prayer and worship. The singing, the praying together, the fellowship – these are at the heart of their Christianity. The building is merely the 'shell' – as one modern hymn describes the place of worship. Unfortunately, there is a theology here that only too easily combines with an aesthetic. Contemporary evangelical worship with its demand for flexible space, extensive equipment for amplification and overhead screens, is leaving us with a legacy of buildings that do little to lift the spirit outside the time of worship itself, and do little for those who are not drawn to this style of worship. The modern evangelical church is often aesthetically displeasing.

Even so, local churches still open their doors for particular occasions if not on a daily basis. The sacred buildings of Britain continue to be places where people may express some of their deepest emotions and articulate some of their most profound hopes and fears. They are places of celebration and commemoration, confession and forgiveness. What would Britain be like if all the sacred buildings were to disappear?

There have been societies in which the churches were either closed or not allowed to play a significant or public role. The former Soviet Union was one such. We know that the birth of children continued to be celebrated, people still married and funerals were held. We also know that many people felt dissatisfied with secular alternatives even though they could not always quite put their finger on the reason why. Perhaps a clue was given by the Russian government spokesman, Gennady Gerasimov, commenting on the fall of the Berlin Wall. He said, 'Man does not live by bread alone.' The sacred buildings of Britain are a continual reminder that we do not live by bread alone. But if the churches were to disappear, what other buildings would remind us of these other needs, the needs of the soul, and what other buildings would remain to meet the need for spiritual nourishing?

Some would. We could argue that this is one of the functions of the theatre. There are parallels between what happens in a church and a theatre. There is something theatrical about liturgy, as the word 'liturgy' itself bears witness. In the theatre, we can be challenged intellectually and stirred emotionally. Great themes of life and death can be explored. But theatres are patronized by the middle and professional classes; vast numbers of British people never enter them. There is a contrast here with the old Soviet Union. The first time I went to the Bolshoi Theatre to see a little-performed ballet I was surrounded by dozens of very excited women of all ages, factory workers from a Moscow suburb whose works outing each year always ended with a visit to the theatre. But even if such a culture existed in Britain, theatres are few and far between and tend to be located in the larger urban centres.

We might argue that the university performs a similar role. It is true that the university invites us to share insights and knowledge and to learn from one another. But it is not a place where we can express grief or disappointment or exuberant joy or make confession – though this might form part of the raw material for research. And if theatres are middle class, universities do not draw from a much bigger range of the population and, in any case, generally only play a role in people's lives for a relatively short period of time. Other public buildings perform very different functions, more related to mammon than the things of the spirit – town halls, law courts, shopping malls and markets. ⁜ In short, sacred buildings are almost unique. They can perform a role which no other public building wholly does in town or village. This accounts for the fact that attempts to close churches can sometimes be met by as much hostility from non-members as members. This suggests that the church has a responsibility not simply to those who worship there faithfully week by week, but to a wider constituency. Churches are, in Philip Larkin's words, serious places on serious earth. They are the one public building set aside to allow for the expression and articulation of all that we mean by 'man does not live by bread alone'. And they are ubiquitous.

In 2004 the State itself rediscovered the importance of ceremony and ritual in marking significant moments in people's lives when it instituted a secular ceremony for making someone a citizen. Whereas in the past most immigrants had become British citizens by making a short declaration at a solicitor's office, now all immigrants to be naturalized are to be invited to a more elaborate ceremony at the local town hall or other public building with as much pomp and ceremony as can be mustered.

From time to time we see the importance of the sacred building in national as well as local life. For instance, it is very hard to know how the coronation of a monarch could be performed in a wholly secular setting. Ritual and ceremony would not be impossible, but they require a greater effort of imagination in buildings designed primarily for other purposes, such as a stadium or concert hall. Who would do the crowning? What would the monarch commit himself to? The language and ritual of liturgy stirs the emotion but allows us greater individual freedom to think our own thoughts than anything a parliamentary sub-committee on 'the arrangements for a non-religious coronation' might come up with.

At the local level we also see the value of the sacred building. Yes, it is possible to welcome children into the world and to celebrate a marriage or a death in a secular setting. But it is more difficult to envisage how the whole range of possibilities offered by the liturgy can be appropriately inserted into such secular occasions. A time for reflection is difficult, though not impossible, but it would be a considerable test to find a secular equivalent to a general confession, still less an absolution, or even an appropriate way of allowing the expression of 'great joy' or 'unimaginable grief'. The secular building and the secular occasion limits the scope for exploring spiritual heights and depths.

From time to time I come across visitors to my church. Some of them leave comments in a visitors' book. I have no way of knowing how many of them are not regular church members; though many are not and say so. Among comments of all kinds were these:

I just wanted somewhere to sit and think.
Thank you for being open.
We appreciated the silence.
'The beauty of holiness.'
I needed to pray.
Your lovely building and the flowers.
I felt God was here.
A house of prayer.
Thank you.
Please pray for Teresa who has leukaemia.

The building is like a sacrament. It is an outward and visible sign of an inward and spiritual grace. We see all the time how important visible signs and physical symbols are for people. New-age religions make use of candles, stones and crystals. When some tragedy occurs people want to light candles or lay flowers. In a similar way, the building helps some people to find God.

Churches should look for imaginative ways of making the building more accessible and helpful to people not just at times of crisis. Here are some suggestions:

- Invite the local secondary school to create a series of stations of the cross which can be displayed around the building during Lent and Holy Week. (If sufficient notice is given, art and design departments will often welcome projects that take them into the community.)
- Invite the local photographic society to illustrate some seasonal theme with an exhibition of photographs – harvest, creation, resurrection.
- Co-operate with local clubs and societies to organize a flower festival with each group being illustrated in a display.

Recognizing the vital role played by sacred buildings in sustaining the spiritual life of members and non-members is the third principle.

Fourth tendency of the contemporary Church:
Move away from the idea of the parish church towards that of the gathered congregation.

Fourth principle for the contemporary Church:
Value and support the concept of the parish church.

All that has been said above points to the need to value the concept of the parish church as opposed to the idea of the gathered congregation.[3] Historically, the Anglican Church has been organized on a geographical basis. The country was divided into parishes served by a local church, which sought to be as inclusive of the Christian community as possible. Parish clergy and their congregations had a care and concern for all the people of a particular area. The parish boundary and not the make-up of the people or the enterprises that were to be found within those boundaries defined the limits of that concern: a parish church, its clergy and congregation would be concerned for Muslims as well as Christians, for shops and offices as well as churches. In contrast, the concerns of the gathered congregation are defined by the interests of the people who happen to make up that congregation. They may or may not have a concern for the people and institutions that happen to be around their place of worship, though even where they do, their overriding objective is to make converts.

The idea of the 'parish church' with its concern for the locality is important in showing to both churchgoers and non-churchgoers what it means to say that the Word became flesh. As far as churchgoers are concerned, it makes them ask hard questions about what it means to apply the gospel in their particular place. Their place may be a rural area with all the problems of second homes or declining farms; it may be a suburban area with all the pressures of commuting and children's schooling; it may be the inner city with its many cultures and many faiths. The commitment to the parishes enables the Church to know these problems and issues at first-hand and forces its members to think about them in the light of the gospel. This will always result in reflection, it will sometimes lead to social action or pastoral concern. As far as non-churchgoers are concerned, the presence of parish churches across the country keeps before people the 'rumour of angels'.

There have been times in the past when the parish model was hard to sustain. At the height of Victorian urban expansion, parish boundaries in the burgeoning cities became seriously out of line with the population. The Church responded with extensive programmes of church building. The task more recently has been twofold: to make bold decisions about the closure of churches marooned in under-populated parts of the inner city while at the same time building (perhaps less permanent) structures elsewhere. One feature of modern house-building has been the desire of increasing numbers of people to move into rural areas. One of the attractions of that is the already existing older village, often with the parish church at its heart. This presents new opportunities.

The role of the parish church has been affected during the course of the twentieth century by changes in British society. The far more diverse nature of modern Britain makes it impossible to claim that only Anglican churches can perform any kind of wider role within local communities – though the history and position of the Anglican Church does continue to offer significant opportunities that may not be available to others. But as the role of the parish church has undergone change, the concept of the parish church as a guiding principle needs to evolve, not be abandoned.

The numerical decline of the Church of England in the twentieth century has led more and more people to give up on the 'parish church' model. In a recent report for the Institute of Contemporary Christianity, Nick Spencer draws parallels between the Church today and the Church in the Dark Ages.[4] He argues that knowledge of Christianity is now, as then, thin among the general population, that there is a confusion of major Christian festivals with all sorts of paganism, and that there is a widespread distrust of institutions. The Church should, therefore, organize itself along the lines of the monastic communities of those early centuries. There should be an abandonment of the 'parish church' model and a concentration on a smaller number of larger congregations that would send out ministers (clergy and laity) into surrounding areas to hold services and undertake pastoral work. This strategy has its attractions, not least because many clergy today are less willing to work in isolation from fellow clergy. Nor is it incompatible with the stance outlined here, provided that the 'thin' faith of the many who are not regular attenders is not dismissed and thought unworthy of being sustained. What cannot be doubted is the need to keep thinking about appropriate strategies for supporting the faith of those large numbers of people who still want to be identified as Christians while not wishing to attend church regularly. Here are some suggestions:

- In the Advent season, invite a local school to contribute pictures for a 'Stations of the Nativity' – and construct carol services around the themes of the pictures.
- Ask a local choral society to help put together an evening of readings and music around a theme – though invite them out of their season for concerts.
- At weddings and baptisms, invite families to contribute photographs to a board showing 'weddings/baptisms this month'
- Consider having a lively Service of the Word early on Saturday evenings for those with children and a more meditative and thoughtful eucharist on Sunday morning.
- Mark all major festivals with very traditional services that appeal to those who want to hear the Christian narrative without too much surrounding commentary. (One person contacted me after a Thought for the Day broadcast to say that he always attended the annual Christmas carol service of lessons and carols in his Derbyshire village because there was no sermon – 'I have no interest in the vicar's speculations,' he said, but he did like to hear the narratives of the Christian faith even though he had the greatest difficulty with the doctrines of the Church. He described himself and his family as 'Anglican sceptics'.)
- Arrange short, lunch-time Christmas carol services for all the 'caring professionals' in the parish.
- Write to all those who have arranged funerals through the church in the previous year and invite them to an annual service of remembrance for the bereaved. Keep the service short and follow it with tea and cakes.

The fourth principle, to value and support the concept of the parish church, is also a shorthand for everything I have argued for throughout these chapters. I believe the Christian churches now stand at crossroads. The tendency and the temptation is to move the Church in the direction of the 'gathered church'. But it is wishful thinking to suppose that this will increase overall participation in Church membership. It does, however, lead to Christians making too sharp a distinction between church and world and the result of that will be to miss opportunities to serve those Christians who are never going to be regular attenders. Ministry will be assimilated to mission and those who do not attend but think of themselves as Christians will ask the Church for bread and receive none.

Notes

1. Sacred hearts: The legacy of Christianity

1 E. A. Down, 'The Tractarian tradition', in N. P. Williams and Charles Harris (editors), *Northern Catholicism*. SPCK, 1933, p. 276.

2 Peter Green, *The Town Parson*. Longmans, Green and Co, 1919, p. 25.

3 H. Cox, *The Secular City*. SCM Press, London, 1965.

4 I was especially influenced by the writing of the British Methodist theologian, the Revd Dr John Vincent and the work of the Urban Theology Unit, Sheffield. See John Vincent, *Secular Christ: A Contemporary Interpretation of Jesus*. Lutterworth Press, 1967.

5 I brought my own concerns to my membership of the Archbishops' Commission on Urban Priority Areas, which led to the report *Faith in The City* in 1985.

6 Alfred, Lord Tennyson, *A Memoir by His Son*. Macmillan, 1899, vol. IV, p. 184. Cited in Ian Bradley, *Abide With Me: the World of Victorian Hymns*. SCM Press, 1997, p. 220.

7 C. Davies, 'Moralization and demoralization: a moral explanation for changes in crime, disorder and social problems', in D. Anderson (editor), *The Loss of Virtue: Moral Confusion and Social Disorder in Britain and America*. Social Affairs Unit, London, 1922, p. 11.

8 The figures as percentages are: Christian 71.8 per cent, Muslim 3 per cent, Hindu 1.1 per cent, Sikh 0.6 per cent, Jewish 0.5 per cent, Buddhist 0.3 per cent, other religious traditions 0.3 per cent. Those who said they had no

religion accounted for 14.8 per cent. Those who declined to answer 7.7 per cent. Census 2001.

9   See Steve Bruce, 'The demise of Christianity in Britain', in Grave Davie, Paul Heelas and Linda Woodhead (editors), *Predicting Religion: Christian, Secular and Alternative Futures.* Ashgate, 2003.

10 Richard Thomas makes some similar observations in *Counting People In: Changing the Way We Think about Membership and the Church.* SPCK, 2003.

11 However, the character of European culture may well begin to change. At the time of writing there are, for example, 15 million Muslims in the European Union, and they have scarcely begun to make their mark.

12 Bradley, *Abide With Me*, p. 217.

13 Typical is this advertisement for a study day at Sheffield University on 24 July 2004: 'Anchored or fettered? Does your spirituality need religion? An open market-place to explore progressive spirituality for the 21st century . . .'.

14 The Registrar General's categories include:
    IIIa non-manual, clerical and minor supervisory
    IIIb skilled manual
    IV   semi-skilled manual
    V   unskilled manual
    The working class are IIIb–V, though some would want to classify IIIa as working class too.

15 Kendal was the subject of a sociological survey by Lancaster University in 2002–2003. The survey, however, was influenced from the beginning by the secularization thesis. Researchers, therefore, measured Sunday church attendance but showed little or no interest in those other occasions when people come to churches in large – and sometimes very large – numbers. No one counted the numbers at Christmas carol services, for example, which have been increasing in recent years. No one thought that the occasional offices were relevant when measuring the influence of religion on people's lives.

2. Secular lives: Ministry in a time of no religion

1 The nature of Soviet Communism as an alternative religion was brought home to me in the late 1960s in Red Square. I had just observed two peasant women crossing themselves repeatedly before the embalmed body of Lenin in his tomb beside the Kremlin – as if these were the relics of a saint. As I emerged from the shrine a procession was crossing the square with a banner that read, 'Lenin lives! Yesterday, Today and Forever!'

2 The poets catch the mood. Alexander Pope told his contemporaries, 'Think not the heavens to scan, The proper study of mankind is man.' This marked the turn from God to the world.

3 For some theological and philosophical reflections on time see: Hugh Rayment-Pickard, *The Myths of Time: from Saint Augustine to American Beauty.* Darton, Longman and Todd, 2004.

4 Frank Furedi, *Therapy Culture: Cultivating Vulnerability in an Uncertain Age.* Routledge, 2004, p. 1.

5 Churches in this tradition need to think carefully about how they may unwittingly be preparing the ground for the turn to the self in a way that leads to the rejection of orthodox Christianity. When that happens in a religious context, simple selfishness awards itself divine approval, as we saw with the scandal of the Nine O'Clock Service at St Thomas, Crookes, Sheffield.

6 'Fathers Matter' was piloted by the South Essex Partnership NHS Trust in 2004 prior to becoming nationally available. The launch was supported by West Ham United Football Club, whose spokesman said that it was important for men to talk more about their feelings. *The Times,* 20 March 2004.

7 Each time a disaster or tragedy occurs now, therapeutic language is used. So, for example, Soham (where two little girls were murdered in August 2002) was said to be a town

in 'trauma'. The government uses therapeutic language increasingly in policy documents that relate to community cohesion, economic regeneration and criminal justice.

8 A psychologist working for the Cardiff and Vale NHS Trust has drawn up a list of self-help books, which local general practitioners now routinely prescribe for patients who display a range of psychological disorders from depression or anxiety to eating disorders and compulsive gambling. The titles include: *10 Days to Great Self-Esteem* and *The Feeling Good Handbook*. *Guardian*, 11 February 2004.

9 Christopher Lasch, *The Culture of Narcissism: American Life in an Age of Diminishing Expectations*. Warner Books, 1979.

10 All noted by Furedi, *Therapy Culture*.

11 Methodist Church in Singapore. Cited in Michael Counsell (editor), *More Prayers for Sundays*. Harper Collins, 1997, p. 151. Reprinted from *NOW* by permission of the Methodist Publishing House.

3. Why people want their babies christened

1 See Gordon Kuhrt, *Believing in Baptism*. Mowbray, 1987.

2 See Michael Perham, *Liturgy Pastoral and Parochial*. SPCK, 1984.

4. Why people get married in church

1 From the Book of Common Prayer.

2 See Jack Goody, *The European Family: An Historico-Anthropological Essay*. Blackwell, 2000.

3 Letter to Diognetus in *Early Christian Writings*, translated by Maxwell Staniforth. Penguin, 1968.

4 At the Council of Trent in 1563, the Roman Catholic Church took the view that a marriage was only valid if it were performed by a priest.

5 Martha Nussbaum, *The Fragility of Goodness: Luck and*

Ethics in Greek Tragedy and Philosophy. Cambridge University Press, 1986. *Love's Knowledge: Essays on Philosophy and Literature.* Oxford University Press, 1990.

6 When canvassing the area for the local Labour Party I was surprised to discover from the electoral registers that there were in fact people who lived together – they had different surnames – including my next door neighbours. We knew them as Mr and Mrs, but this was a pretence. They were unmarried.

7 There seems to be a considerable market for books that look back wistfully to this time. Examples of recent bestsellers would be: Lorna Sage, *Bad Blood: A Memoir.* Fourth Estate, 2000; William Woodruff, *The Road to Nab End: An Extraordinary Northern Childhood.* Abacus, 1999.

8 The 1960s were a crucial time of change as I argued in a previous book, *Dying and Grieving: A Guide to Pastoral Ministry.* SPCK, 2002.

9 See Helen Oppenheimer, *Marriage.* Mowbray, 1990.

10 Duncan Dormor, 'Come live with me and be my love': marriage, cohabitation and the Church, in Duncan Dormor, Jack McDonald and Jeremy Caddick (editors), *Anglicanism: The Answer to Modernity.* Continuum, 2003, p. 130.

11 *Alternative Service Book*, 1980. Hodder and Stoughton, 1980, p. 288.

12 *Common Worship: Pastoral Services.* The Archbishops' Council, 2000, p. 105.

13 A thoughtful church report on cohabitation is *Cohabitation: A Christian Reflection*, Diocese of Southwark, 2002.

14 This is argued for in Anthony Giddens, *The Transformation of Intimacy: Sexuality, Love and Eroticism in Modern Societies.* Polity Press, 1992.

15 *Independent*, 16 July 2003.

16 Confetti.co.uk – *Daily Telegraph*, 9 July 2003.

17 One perplexed husband-to-be said, 'Why have we come to church to get married? Isn't that what churches are for? If

we wanted a book we would go to the library.'

18 See *Does Marriage Matter?* Civitas: The Institute for the Study of Civil Society (The Mezzanine, Elizabeth House, 39 York Road, London SE1 7NQ).

19 It is known that, statistically, marriage reduces criminality whereas cohabiting increases it. The argument is that marriage causes men in particular to alter their behaviour and become more responsible, eschewing antisocial and criminal behaviour. See John H. Lamb and Robert J. Sampson, *Shared Beginnings, Divergent Lives*. Harvard University Press, 2004.

5. Why funerals are overwhelmingly Christian

1 The changes are described in detail in Tony Walter, *The Revival of Death*, Routledge, 1994. See also the early chapters of my *Dying and Grieving*, SPCK, 2002.

2 In 1988 7 per cent of all deaths were in hospices.

3 The point is made by Frank Furedi in *Therapy Culture*, pp. 19f.

4 I was involved helping relatives and friends of those bereaved by the Hillsborough Football disaster. Afterwards, counselling was offered not only to those who witnessed the deaths and relatives of those who died; it was subsequently also offered to those who had counselled them!

5 Edith Olivier, *The Love Child*. Virago Modern Classics, 1981, p. 19.

6 Wesley Carr, *Brief Encounters*. SPCK, 1985.

7 *Common Worship: Pastoral Services*, p. 5.

8 *Book of Common Order of the Church of Scotland*. St Andrew Press, 1994, p. 319.

9 See Alan Billings, *Dying and Grieving*, p. 158.

10 Peter Singer, *Rethinking Life and Death: The Collapse of our Traditional Ethics*. Oxford University Press, 1994, p. 190. Similar views have been expressed by Professor

John Harris, a member of the British Medical Association's Ethics Committee. Professor Harris believes that if it is morally possible to abort a foetus it is morally possible to kill a child. He is quoted as saying, 'I don't think infanticide is always unjustifiable. I don't think it is plausible to think that there is any moral change that occurs during the journey down the birth canal.' *Sunday Telegraph*, 25 January 2004.

6. Conclusions

1 For an example of this in a North American context, see R. Stephen Warner, *New Wine in Old Wineskins: Evangelicals and Liberals in a Small-Town Church*. University of California, 1988.

2 Similar arguments can be found in Richard Thomas, *Counting People In*.

3 This is discussed in Giles Ecclestone (editor), *A Parish Church? Explorations in the Relationship of the Church and the World*. Mowbray, 1988.

4 Nick Spencer, *Parochial Vision*. London Institute of Contemporary Christianity and Jubilee Centre, 2004.

Index

LE 02/08